C000263143

UK AIRFIELDS

The Harrier GR5A equips Wittering's No 1 Squadron and the base's other unit, No 233 OCU, is equipped with the GR3, GR5 and T4 variants, exemplified here by GR3 XV744 '3K'.
Jonathan Falconer

abc

UK MILITARY AIRFIELDS

Jonathan Falconer & Wal Gandy

IAN ALLAN
Publishing

CONTENTS

First published 1992

ISBN 0 7110 2055 8

Published by Ian Allan Ltd, Shepperton, Surrey; and printed by Ian Allan Printing Ltd at their works at Coombelands in Runnymede, England.

ACKNOWLEDGEMENTS

The authors would like to thank the following individuals for their help in the preparation of this book: Dave Braithwaite, Annie Gronow, John Dunnell, Paul Jackson, Andrew March, Daniel March, Peter R. March, Mike Powney, Brian Strickland and Wg Cdr A.E.P. Webb AFC, RAF.

1. INTRODUCTION

Airfields have made a significant impact on the appearance of the 20th century English landscape. By the end of World War 2 more than 550 military airfields had been constructed across the UK, the majority for use by the RAF. Many of these were of a temporary nature, for hostilities only, which were closed for good soon after the war ended. But many of the more substantial airfields, whose origins lay in the huge prewar Expansion Scheme, survive to this day. Take the old bomber stations of Waddington and Wyton, for example. Once upon a time their taxiways and runways reverberated to the throaty roar of Rolls-Royce Merlin-powered Lancaster and Mosquito bombers heading into the dusky skies bound for Germany. Today, these airfields are just as accommodating towards their newer charges — the Tornados, Canberras, Hawks, Sentries and Nimrods of Strike Command.

In the 1990s, the UK offers both the aviation enthusiast and casual observer alike an opportunity to visit many of the military airfields that are scattered across the national landscape. Whether one's visit is simply parking the car along the main road bordering an active airfield, as with the A1065 which runs beside RAF Lakenheath in Suffolk; or as a paying guest at a Battle of Britain 'at Home' day or summer air display, an interesting and photographically rewarding day out can be had.

Some military airfields have special enclosures outside the perimeter fence set aside for enthusiasts to watch the comings and goings. RAF Mildenhall in Suffolk is one such example. At others it is possible to find a good vantage point at the roadside, close to the main runway threshold or near to Hardened Aircraft Shelter complexes. In the UK, military authorities are fairly tolerant of the camera-toting notebook-wielding enthusiast fraternity who poke all manner of camera lenses and binoculars through the mesh of airfield perimeter fences in their insatiable thirst for the 'right gen'. But when visiting the perimeter of a military airfield there are a number of golden rules which should always be borne in mind:

● 1. Park your vehicle in such a way as not to cause a hazard to other road users or pedestrians.

● 2. Military airfields are defence establishments. Their personnel and aircraft are tasked with the serious business of defending the nation against aggressors.

● 3. Contrary to the views of some enthusiasts, these airfields and their resident aircraft do not exist solely for the benefit of spotters, photographers or casual observers.

● 4. Military airfields have perimeter fences and gates for security purposes. They keep out unwelcome intruders. Some may even tell you they keep in unwilling airmen! Do not interfere with these fences or gates.

● 5. In the event of an accident on or around the airfield, emergency services may need access to crash gates. Do not obstruct these gates with vehicles at any time.

● 6. Do not trespass. If, in the furtherance of your interest, you force entry to an airfield then you are breaking the law and will become liable to arrest by military authorities, risking prosecution under the Official Secrets Act.

These guidelines may seem like simple common sense. That is because they are. In the heat of the moment they are all too often forgotten when pursuing a taxiing Tornado around the airfield perimeter at Coningsby, camera at the ready! Respect these common sense guidelines and your visit will be all the more agreeable to you, your fellow enthusiasts and the military authorities.

2. HOW TO USE THIS BOOK

Listed alphabetically in the following pages you will find 48 airfields in current use by the British Army (ARMY), Ministry of Defence (Procurement Executive) (MOD [PE]), Royal Air Force (RAF), Royal Navy (RN) and United States Air Forces Europe (USAFE); civil airfields or airports with some military operations flown from them (CIVIL); or military aircraft manufacturers' airfields (BAe). The airfield's name and county are followed by its owner/operator, International Civil Aviation Organisation (ICAO) location code, and main switchboard telephone number. For example: WYTON, Cambridgeshire

(RAF) EGUY Tel: 0480 52451. A brief operational history of the airfield is then given followed by details of current user squadrons and units, and finally advice about the best places for viewing aircraft activities on the airfield. At the end of the main section you will find a brief A to Z of airfields offering minor military aircraft activity.

3. AIRFIELD INFRASTRUCTURE

All military airfields in use in the UK today can trace their origins back at least to World War 2, the prewar Expansion Scheme period, even some to World War 1 and earlier.

● **RUNWAYS**: A triangular three-runway system was generally favoured for the majority of the RAF's airfields during World War 2, particularly those of Bomber Command. All airfields built from 1940 onwards were constructed with paved runways and taxiways using concrete and Tarmac. The main runway used for take-offs and landings was invariably along a NE/SW axis to take advantage of the prevailing wind. These runways could cope fairly well with the performance demands of the Mosquito and Lancaster, but when it came to the postwar generation of jet aircraft with far greater performance abilities and all-up weights, not to mention scorching afterburners, the runways were found wanting.

Consequently, the years following World War 2 saw extensive building work to lengthen runways at a number of airfields across the UK, for example at Waddington where the main runway was extended to 3,000yd. More land was acquired in order to extend the main runways, leaving the remaining two as subsidiaries; in many cases, these subsidiaries have become completely superfluous to requirements.

New types of runway surfacing materials continue to be developed in order to provide greater tensile strength and better adhesion for the wheel-tyres of today's high performance aircraft. To minimise the risk of accidental damage to aircraft or runways through misuse, runway strengths are generally referred to in official Service manuals by the Load Classification Group (LCG) system. This relates to the bearing strength of a particular station's runway, derived from its sub-grade characteristics and type of construction. Each LCG embraces a range of Load Classification Numbers (LCN) which correspond with the types of aircraft that can use a particular runway. For example, an LCN of 10 and under corresponds with an LCG of VII. This means that only the lighter types of aircraft with gross weights of 10,000lb and under can use this runway. An LCN of 101-120 (ie, 101,000-120,000lb gross weight) corresponds with an LCG of I, for the heaviest aircraft.

There are a number of other classifications which show the gross aircraft weight which can be accepted for continuous operation, by referring to maximum tyre pressure, or undercarriage configuration. For example, single wheel-type undercarriage (F-15 Eagle), single tandem-type (C-130 Hercules) and twin delta tandem-type (C-5A Galaxy).

Some runways are equipped with aircraft arresting systems, limited by the specific engagement weight and speed criteria based on the structural restrictions of individual aircraft, and on the arresting system's own limitations. These systems range from rotary hydraulic, chain arresting and spray arresting gear, to barrier arresting systems.

● **HANGARS**: Wartime hangars can still be seen and in use at many of the UK's operational airfields. For example, C Type (1934) at Binbrook, Finningley, Leeming, Leuchars, Waddington and Wittering; T Type (1941-43) at St Mawgan and Yeovilton; and Bellman (1937) at St Athan.

Used primarily for major overhauls, servicing and storage, hangars have crew rooms and flight offices in single or two-storey annexes built along the length of their external walls. Access to these can be gained either from inside the hangar or by external doors.

● **HARDENED AIRCRAFT SHELTERS (HAS)**: These are like mini hangars, providing combat aircraft with a secure environment which is resistant to blast damage from either conventional or nuclear weapons. They are unable, however, to withstand a direct hit. All RAF and USAFE frontline fighters and bombers are housed in HAS complexes. One aircraft and its crew can both live and fight from a HAS in wartime. In peacetime, up to two aircraft can be housed in one shelter, although they cannot both be started up together. The first aircraft must leave the shelter before the second crew can board and start up.

Because of the UK's geographical location in Europe — ie, furthest from forces of the former Warsaw Pact — priority for the provision of HAS went to NATO airfields in continental Europe. The UK's HAS programme was financed by NATO and commenced in 1982.

● **'Q' SHEDS**: Quick Reaction Alert (QRA) Sheds, or 'Q' Sheds for short, are simple aircraft shelters with rooves, open at both ends, and intended for use by fighter aircraft. They are positioned at the end of a runway where a pair of fighters and their crews can shelter whilst maintaining a 10min continuous readiness, in order to intercept potentially hostile incursions into UK airspace. Although largely superseded by HAS, crews still talk about being on 'Q'.

● **CONTROL TOWERS**: These important airfield flying control buildings are often adapted from World War 2-vintage brick watchtowers which were built to a number of different Air Ministry specifications. Recent additions include extensions and additions of glazed cupolas for improved vision atop the existing structure as, for example, at Linton-on-Ouse; or completely new designs, as at Leeming — nicknamed the 'Happy Eater' because of its striking resemblance to the road houses of the same name.

● **AIRFIELD LANDING & NAVIGATION AIDS**: Most UK military airfields are equipped with one or more of the following navigation aids:

● **Aerodrome Beacons** — Alternating white/green or flashing white lights, normally located only at civil airfields;

● **Identification Beacons** — These exhibit a Morse group of one or more letters every 12sec. Civil airfields show a white light, military airfields red. For example, Brize Norton's identification beacon codeletters are 'BZ', in red;

● **Instrument Landing System (ILS)** — Bearings and distances are given automatically to the aircraft from Outer Markers to Runway Threshold;

● **Non-Directional Beacons (NDB)** — Civil airfields with NDBs use them as approach aids or as passive navigational waypoints;

● **TACAN** (TACtical Air Navigation Equipment);

● **DME** (Distance Measuring Equipment);

● **VOR** (Very-high-frequency Omni-Range);

● **THE BAe HARRIER and SEA HARRIER**: Although the RAF's UK-based Harrier squadrons are assigned to RAF Wittering in peacetime, during times of international tension or war they would deploy to dispersed sites and forward airstrips in the field. Similarly, FAA Sea Harriers are assigned to RNAS Yeovilton in peacetime, with periodic deployments aboard the Royal Navy's three carriers, *Ark Royal*, *Illustrious* and *Invincible*. Depending upon the war scenario, they might operate from conventional airfields or from carriers. The RAF's Harrier force is also capable of operating from RN carriers, as witnessed during the Falklands conflict in 1982.

4. THE RAF'S ROLE IN NATO

The North Atlantic Treaty was signed in Washington on 4 April 1949, as a defensive response by Western powers to the escalation in the Cold War, by representatives of Great Britain, France, Belgium, the Netherlands, Luxembourg, Canada and the USA. Denmark, Iceland, Italy, Norway and Portugal were also officially invited to accede to the Treaty. Greece and Turkey joined in 1952 and West Germany in 1955. The resulting North Atlantic Treaty Organisation (NATO) is essentially a common defence system for the North Atlantic area and Article V of the Treaty provides that an armed attack against one or more of the parties shall be considered an attack against all. A consequence of the formation of NATO was the birth, on 14 May 1955, of the Warsaw Pact, a military alliance formed by the Soviet Union, Albania, Bulgaria, Czechoslovakia, East Germany, Hungary, Poland and Romania. This Treaty was the communist answer to the formation of NATO and the re-militarisation of West Germany. In the event of war, forces of the other Pact countries would have become operationally subordinate to the Soviet Union. As a result of the recent break-up of the communist system in Eastern Europe, the Warsaw Pact was officially dissolved in 1991, although the NATO structure still remains.

As a member of NATO, Great Britain's armed forces would be compelled to play a central role in any future conflict by virtue of the nation's geographical location. A large number of RAF and US strike aircraft are based at airfields in eastern and central England; a proportion of US and British reinforcements for the NATO Central Front in Europe would fly from transport airfields in England. Because of this strong commitment to NATO's total strike capability, the Soviet Union would have found it difficult to ignore the UK's central role in the Alliance. Therefore, the UK needed to plan a solid defence of the homeland to protect it against attack and to provide a safe base from which to expedite its NATO role.

Put very simply, and with specific reference to the RAF's airborne commitment to NATO and home defence, the RAF's home-based Groups provide seven operational

functions, all but one of which are vital to NATO: air defence of UK air space with the Tornado F3 and Phantom FGR2 (No 11 Group); strike-attack in NATO offensive operations with the Tornado GR1, Buccaneer S2B, Jaguar GR1A and Harrier GR5, GR7, Nimrod R1P and ECM Canberra (Nos 1 and 18 Groups); strategic and tactical reconnaissance with the Tornado GR1A, Jaguar GR1A and Canberra (Nos 1 and 18 Groups); air-to-air refuelling, strategic and tactical transport support with the TriStar K1/KC1, VC10 C1/K2/K3, Victor K2, Hercules C1P/C3P, HS125, Andover C1/CC2, Chinook HC1, Puma HC1, Wessex HC2 (No 1 Group); maritime patrol with the Nimrod MR2/MR2P (No 18 Group); airborne early warning for the UK Air Defence Region and NATO with the Boeing E-3D AEW1 Sentry (No 11 Group); and search and rescue with the Sea King HAR3 and Wessex HC2 (No 18 Group). On the NATO Central Front in Europe, RAF Germany provides comprehensive air support, but this role is outside the scope of this book.

5. WHY USAF UNITS ARE BASED IN THE UK

US military aircraft and personnel have been stationed in the UK ever since 1942, from where they flew offensive operations against Nazi Germany during World War 2. With the dawn of victory for the Allies in 1945, USAAF units withdrew from their UK bases but returned in 1948 with the growing tension in Berlin and the ensuing blockade. In 1951, with the rapid escalation of the Cold War, the US 3rd Air Force was activated to co-ordinate all USAF activities in the UK and ever since then it has maintained a significant presence here.

Although they are technically RAF bases, each of which is under the command of an RAF officer (who are actually liaison officers), US bases in the UK are staffed and operated by USAF personnel under the overall control of the 3rd Air Force, US Air Forces Europe (USAFE) from its UK HQ at RAF Mildenhall in Suffolk.

The continued presence in the UK of US forces is based on the informal Truman-Churchill Agreement of January 1952, and the Visiting Forces Act of 30 October 1952. The US continues to decline to publish the text of the Agreement, although a Press statement issued in 1952 stated:

'Under arrangements made for the common defense, the United States has the use of certain bases in the United Kingdom. We reaffirm the understanding that the use of the bases in an emergency would be a matter for joint decision by His Majesty's Government and the United States' Government in the light of the circumstances prevailing at the time.'

The main USAF bases in the UK are currently Alconbury, Bentwaters/Woodbridge (the latter due for closure in 1992), Greenham Common, Lakenheath, Mildenhall and Upper Heyford. Their primary role, until the recent changes in Eastern Europe and the Soviet Union, was in support of NATO ground forces on the Central European Front or deep strike missions into Warsaw Pact territory with conventional or nuclear weapons.

Other roles which the USAF plays with a more obvious application to the immediate defence of the UK include air defence, air-to-air refuelling, tactical airlift, airborne command and control, tactical and strategic reconnaissance, and search and rescue.

The stationing of US forces on British soil has a number of advantages to Britain: an attack on Europe would mean an attack on US forces, thus ensuring their participation in any European war; Britain has a say in US nuclear planning; the close relationship with the US enables Britain to gain access to US intelligence and military hardware.

However, with the break-up of the Warsaw Pact which began late in 1989, and the ongoing process of fragmentation and democratisation in what was the Soviet Union, initiated by Mikhail Gorbachev and Boris Yeltsin, the role of the USAF in the UK and continental Europe must now be redefined.

6. POWER IN THE BALANCE

The year 1991 witnessed two of the most significant events in 20th century history: the break-up of the Warsaw Pact and the dramatic disintegration, after almost 70 years, of the Soviet Union, the world's second superpower, culminating in the Treaty of Alma Ata on 21 December.

The heads of 11 Soviet republics gathered at Alma Ata, the capital of Kazakhstan, to endorse and extend the commonwealth founded by Russia, Ukraine and Belorussia 11 days before. Russia, headed by Boris Yeltsin, has been acknowledged as leader of a voluntary 'Commonwealth of Independent States', heir to the USSR's international status and its place in the UN Security Council.

The Treaty's agreed points include joint command of strategic nuclear forces and a strict non-proliferation policy. However, the question of what to do with the conventional armed forces is a harder issue to resolve, particularly to Russia's satisfaction. Ukraine and Azerbaijan would like to have their own armed forces, whereas Russia favours the idea of a single army, navy and air force under central command.

With this wholesale dismantling of the Soviet war machine, the argument against a US military presence in the UK gains credence in as much as it no longer serves our national interest. Many cornerstones of the West's postwar defence policies were built upon the threat of a Warsaw Pact/Soviet Union attack on NATO forces in Europe, but all this must now be reappraised. Proposals and counterproposals on conventional and nuclear arms cuts from Washington and Moscow are sure to lead to a major change in the strategic balance between East and West. Ironically, the new state of Russia has also intimated a future desire to join NATO, although this will obviously become an issue for some detailed, and doubtless lengthy, negotiations.

With events on the world stage moving so quickly, it is difficult to predict the future role of USAF units in the UK. There may well be a reduction in the establishment of aircraft and personnel, perhaps even a total withdrawal. But with the speed of change in international relations that we have witnessed since 1989, it would be inappropriate to make any firm pronouncements on what role, if any, USAFE will play in the defence of Europe in the 1990s.

It should also be borne in mind that we, as a society, are still a long way from enjoying a world free from threats of violence. There is concern amongst NATO member states about who now controls the vast arsenal of nuclear weaponry in the new states of the Commonwealth of Independent States. The fate of such a powerful force and, more critically, who has 'the finger on the button', needs very careful monitoring. There are real fears of political destabilisation within these new states which are equally as prone to democratic trends as they are to renewed authoritarianism or, indeed, anarchy.

The August coup in Moscow during 1991 shows that there are still sinister forces at work within the old Soviet hierarchy, determined to reverse the recent radical changes in the East, thereby securing a return to the Cold War mentality of the 'Old Order' in the Kremlin. But what, also, will be the long-term result of a shift in the balance of power in favour of the USA? What, also, of the resurgence of a powerful and united Germany?

The leading article in *The Times* of 23 December 1991 concluded with a strong warning to us all: 'From the Oder to the Urals there is now one of the great vacuums of the twentieth century. All eyes should focus on Bonn as well as Moscow. The old democracies are now to be tested as severely as the new ones.' Let us hope, bearing in mind their leading roles in two cataclysmic World Wars this century, that neither nation is found to be wanting in the ways of peace.

ABBREVIATIONS

A&AEE	Aircraft & Armament Experimental Establishment
AAC	Army Air Corps
AAF	Army Air Force
ACCS	Airborne Command & Control Squadron
ADV	Advanced
AEF	Air Experience Flight
AEW	Airborne Early Warning
AES	Air Engineering School
AFB	Air Force Base
AETW	Air Engineering Training Wing
AGA	Army Gliding Association
AIB	Accident Investigation Bureau
ALW	Airlift Wing
ANG	Air National Guard
ARRS	Aerospace Rescue & Recovery Squadron
ASUW	Anti-SUrface Warfare
ASW	Anti-Submarine Warfare
AWACS	Airborne Warning & Control System
BBMF	Battle of Britain Memorial Flight
BDRF	Battle Damage Repair Flight
BFWF	Basic Fixed-Wing Flight
C&M	Care & Maintenance
CFS	Central Flying School
DACT	Dissimilar Air Combat Training
DME	Distance Measuring Equipment
EAP	Experimental Aircraft Programme
ECS	Electronic Countermeasures Squadron
ECW	Electronic Countermeasures Wing
ELG	Emergency Landing Ground
EFTS	Elementary Flying Training Squadron
ETPS	Empire Test Pilots' School
FAA	Fleet Air Arm
FACF	Forward Air Control Flight
FBS	Fighter Bomber Squadron
FBW	Fighter Bomber Wing
Flt	Flight
FRADU	Fleet Requirements & Air Direction Unit
FTS	Flying Training School
FS	Fighter Squadron
FW	Fighter Wing
Grp	Group
HAS	Hardened Aircraft Shelter
HMS	His/Her Majesty's Ship
IAT	International Air Tattoo
ILS	Instrument Landing System
JBG	Jagdbombergeschwader
LCG	Load Classification Group
LCN	Load Classification Number
MAC	Military Airlift Command
MEDA	Military Emergency Diversion Aerodrome
MOD	Ministry of Defence
MOD(PE)	Ministry of Defence Procurement Executive
MR	Maritime Reconnaissance
MU	Maintenance Unit
NAS	Naval Air Station
NDB	Non-Directional Beacon
OCU	Operational Conversion Unit
OEU	Operational Evaluation Unit
OTU	Operational Training Unit
PRU	Photographic Reconnaissance Unit
QRA	Quick Reaction Alert
RAE	Royal Aerospace Establishment
RAFGSA	Royal Air Force Gliding & Soaring Association
RLG	Relief Landing Ground
RNAS	Royal Naval Air Station/Royal Naval Air Service
SAC	Strategic Air Command
SAOEU	Strike Attack Operational Evaluation Unit
SAR	Search-and-Rescue
SAH	School of Aircraft Handling
SKTU	Sea King Training Unit
SOS	Special Operations Squadron
SoTT	School of Technical Training
SOW	Special Operations Wing
SRW	Strategic Reconnaissance Wing
STOL	Short Take-Off & Landing
STOVL	Short Take-Off & Vertical Landing
TACAN	TACtical Air Navigation
TFS	Tactical Fighter Squadron (historic title)
TFW	Tactical Fighter Wing (historic title)
TMTS	Trade Management Training School
TTTE	Trinational Tornado Training Establishment
TWU	Tactical Weapons Unit
TWCU	Tornado Weapons Conversion Unit
UAS	University Air Squadron
UKADR	United Kingdom Air Defence Region
USAF	United States Air Force
USAFE	United States Air Force Europe
USAAF	United States Army Air Force
USN	United States Navy
VGS	Volunteer Gliding Squadron
VOR	Very-high-frequency Omni-Range

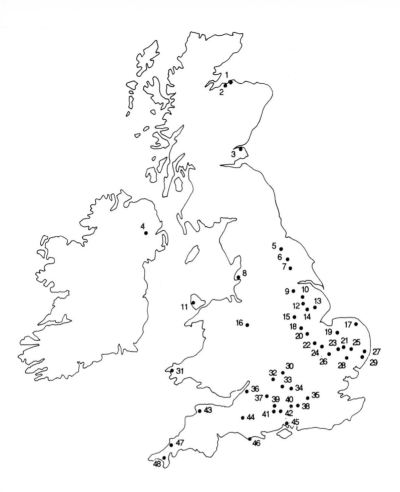

1 Lossiemouth	17 Coltishall	33 Abingdon
2 Kinloss	18 Cottesmore	34 Benson
3 Leuchars	19 Marham	35 Northolt
4 Aldergrove (Belfast Airport)	20 Wittering	36 Filton
5 Leeming	21 Lakenheath	37 Lyneham
6 Linton-on-Ouse	22 Alconbury	38 Farnborough
7 Church Fenton	23 Mildenhall	39 Netheravon
8 Warton	24 Wyton	40 Odiham
9 Finningley	25 Honington	41 Boscombe Down
10 Scampton	26 Teversham (Cambridge Airport)	42 Middle Wallop
11 Valley	27 Bentwaters	43 Chivenor
12 Waddington	28 Wattisham	44 Yeovilton
13 Coningsby	29 Woodbridge	45 Lee-on-Solent
14 Cranwell	30 Upper Heyford	46 Portland
15 Syerston	31 Brawdy	47 St Mawgan (Newquay Airport)
16 Shawbury	32 Brize Norton	48 Culdrose

ABINGDON

Berks (RAF) EGUD Tel: 0235 521288

This RAF base is situated to the northwest of the town of Abingdon, west of the A34(T) dual carriageway, north of the A415, and east of the A420/A338. There are minor roads around the perimeter of the site and from these good views of the — usually infrequent — movements can be observed. There are two operational runways: 18/36 runs south/north and is 6,534ft long; 08/26 runs roughly east/west and is 4,800ft long.

Abingdon originally opened as a bomber station in 1932 and was upgraded in 1936 in accordance with the RAF's prewar Expansion Scheme plans. From the outbreak of war in 1939 until the spring of 1940, Abingdon hosted the Whitleys of Nos 97 and 166 Squadrons but then it settled down to its wartime role as a bomber Operational Training Unit, hosting No 10 OTU with Whitleys and Wellingtons under the control of No 91 Group until in 1946 Transport Command took over control of Abingdon. A long affiliation with the RAF's worldwide transport commitment followed with such famous types as the Dakota, York, Hastings, Beverley and Andover flying the world's military air routes until in 1976 major flying operations ceased when control of the station passed to RAF Support Command.

Sadly, Abingdon is better known today for its inactivity and has been earmarked for closure by the spring of 1993*. At present it stores ex-British Airways Type 1151 Super VC-10 airliners, pending their conversion to the airborne tanker role for the RAF, and RAF Nimrod aircraft from the aborted AEW3 conversion programme. However, these airframes are slowly being dispersed to duties elsewhere, or for conversion to the airborne tanker role as originally intended.

Abingdon was also home to the RAF's Jaguar and Hawk Maintenance Units (MU) where routine major overhauls to these aircraft is carried out. These have now transferred to St Athan. Also based here is the RAF's Battle Damage Repair Flight (BDRF) which acts as the training unit for instructors who are allocated to other bases within the Service to oversee running repairs to damaged aircraft serving with operational squadrons. Static airframes used for patching and repairs are situated in the northeast corner of the airfield and can be seen from

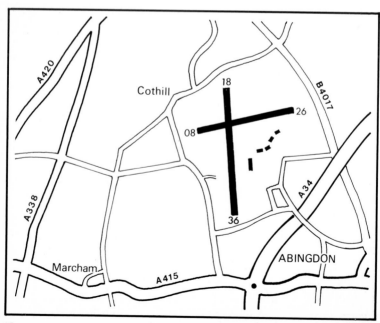

Super-VC10 aircraft are stored at Abingdon, pending their conversion by British Aerospace (BAe) to the air-to-air refuelling role. *Peter R. March (PRM)*

the north side perimeter road. There is currently one Hunter aircraft on display at the main gate as Gate Guardian, to be found west from the B4017 road.

The RAF Exhibition Flight is also based here and takes its real and replica airframes by road to air shows and events all over the country as an aid to recruiting and Service publicity.

There are two types of active aircraft currently based here: the Bulldog T1 trainer with London University Air Squadron (UAS) and Oxford UAS; and the older Chipmunk trainer with No 6 Air Experience Flight (AEF). These are most often to be found flying at weekends. The units are due to rede-

ploy to Benson (qv) following Abingdon's closure in 1993.

Vantage points for photography depend upon which runway is in use, but the minor roads on the north, west and south sides of the airfield perimeter offer scope. However, the best time to view the station's activities is on the annual RAF 'at Home' day during September. The 1990 event was particularly auspicious because the Battle of Britain 50th Anniversary Flypast overflew here en-route from Buckingham Palace - a massed display of over 160 aircraft.

*Latest information is that RAF Abingdon will close on 31 July 1992.

ALCONBURY

Cambridgeshire (USAFE) EGWZ Tel: 0480 822383/823740 OS Map Ref: TL20/76
This busy air base is situated to the north-west of Huntingdon, between the A1/A14 to the west, and the British Rail main line to the east. There is only one operational runway, 12/30, which is 9,009ft long.

Alconbury began life in 1938 as a satellite airfield for Upwood in No 2 Group

Bomber Command, operating Fairey Battles. With the outbreak of war it was transferred to the control of nearby Wyton (qv) and hosted three squadrons at various times, with Blenheims and Wellingtons, until it was transferred to the USAAF in August 1942. B-24 Liberator and B-17 Flying Fortress bomb groups of the 8th AF were then stationed at Alconbury, flying daylight

13

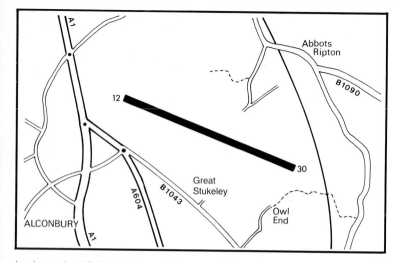

bomber and pathfinding missions until the end of the war when they returned to the USA. Under RAF control again, Alconbury underwent a major rebuilding programme and then in 1953 the USAF returned to make Alconbury its major UK air base for tactical fighter and reconnaissance missions.

Today, Alconbury is operated by the United States Air Forces in Europe (USAFE). At the time of writing, two very different units are based here with two equally different types of aircraft. The larger of the two (which arrived in August 1987) is the 10th Fighter Wing (FW), with some 38 Fairchild A-10A Thunderbolt IIs. The type is

Unique U-2R Ready Hangars are provided at Alconbury with horizontally folding doors. *Paul Jackson*

well known for its lack of pulchritude and is colloquially known as the Warthog. The other unit is No 95 Reconnaissance Squadron (which arrived in February 1983) and has about 12 Lockheed TR-1A high-altitude reconnaissance 'spy' aircraft based here at any one time. The TR-1 is the successor to the U-2 of Gary Powers' fame, and the occasional U-2 may still be seen here in transit between the USA and Akrotiri.

Aircraft of the 10th FW are allocated to the 509th Fighter Squadron (FS) with grey/white squadron markings at the top of the tailfins.

The 509th FS aircraft are based in Hardened Aircraft Shelters (HAS) at the west end of the base, south of the runway. These may be observed from the perimeter fence at the top of the grass embankment by the B1043, along which there are a couple of discrete parking places suitable for no more than a brief pause.

More A-10A aircraft are housed in HAS on the north side of the runway but to these there is no easy access for viewing.

TR-1 aircraft have individual HAS on the north side of the runway, in the area immediately to the west of the no through-road which leads south to a crash gate from the B1090, just west of the railway bridge, where that road crosses over the railway line.

Plans are in motion for the 10th FW to have completed the withdrawal of its A-10s from Alconbury by the summer of 1992. The unit will be replaced by the 21st and 67th SOS's MH-53J 'Pave Low III' and HC-130N/P Combat Rescue Hercules from Woodbridge (qv). The 7th SOS is also scheduled in mid-1992 to move to Alconbury from Rhein Main, Germany, with its MC-130E 'Combat Talon I' Hercules. This will mean that all USAFE's European special operations units will be positioned at the same base for the first time.

The camp's main gate is on the B1043 road near Great Stukeley, and is still 'guarded' by a full-size plastic replica of an F-5E Tiger II, an aircraft type no longer based here. Other aircraft types, belonging to other NATO air arms, can often be seen visiting Alconbury. For example, KC-135 Stratotankers on weather diversion from Mildenhall, or C-130 Hercules in transit or on deployment. Periodic NATO practice exercises can generate many visitors from overseas air forces.

To observe and photograph movements, the optimum spot is from the south side of the runway at the east end. Access is gained by leaving the B1043 along the minor road signposted Owl End or, at its other end, from the minor road between Huntingdon and Abbots Ripton, where the track is signposted as Bridleway to Great Stukeley; where it crosses the railway line is an excellent spot to observe two forms of transport at the same time!

ALDERGROVE

Co Antrim (RAF) EGAA Tel: 08494 22051
OS Map Ref: J15/80

RAF Aldergrove is situated on the A57 road, 16 miles west of Belfast and three miles east of Lough Neagh. There are two runways which the RAF shares with the civil authorities operating Belfast International Airport: the main is 07/25 which is 9,111ft long; the subsidiary is 17/35, at 6,401ft long.

Aldergrove's history goes back to 1918 when it opened as No 16 Aircraft Acceptance Park, although closed in 1919 it was retained by the RAF for annual exercises. During the interwar years a number of RAF squadrons formed here and at the outbreak of war the station housed No 3 Bombing & Gunnery School, which disbanded in July 1940, and No 23 Maintenance Unit which had arrived in November 1939. July 1940 saw a Fighter Sector HQ set up here and

No 245 Squadron and its Hurricanes moved in for the air defence of Belfast. Several Coastal Command squadrons were detached to Aldergrove on shipping escort and anti-submarine patrol duties until, in July 1941, Fighter Command left and the station was taken over by Coastal Command. For the duration of the war, Aldergrove's various resident squadrons operated the Wellington, Hudson, Liberator, Fortress, Gladiator, Hurricane and Halifax on anti-submarine and Met sorties out over the lonely wastes of the Atlantic Ocean. Postwar, the station maintained a maritime flavour with Halifax, Hastings and Shackleton aircraft engaged on Met flights and maritime patrol duties. In September 1963, Aldergrove became Belfast Airport and in 1978 No 23 MU finally disbanded.

Today, Aldergrove is home to the Wessex HC2 helicopters of No 72 Squadron which has been resident here since November 1981, flying Army support duties over Ulster. No 7 Squadron has a detachment here comprising two CH-47D Chinook helicopters, and about 12 Puma HC1 helicopters, from Nos 33 and 230 Squadrons, regularly operate from here. Also based here is No 665 Squadron AAC, equipped with Gazelle and Lynx helicopters, and No 1 Flight, Northern Ireland Regiment, with the Islander. Gazelle and Lynx helicopters of Ballykelly-based No 655 Squadron regularly operate from/visit Aldergrove.

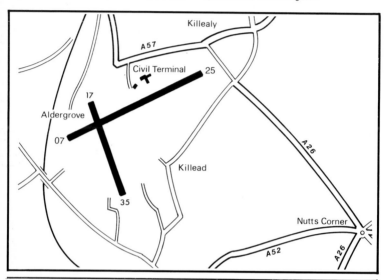

BENSON

Oxfordshire (RAF) EGUB Tel: 0491 37766
OS Map Ref: SU63/90

RAF Benson lies to the southeast of Benson village, northeast of Wallingford. The A423 road from Oxford to Henley-on-Thames passes close to the airfield on its western side; a layby opposite the minor road to Preston Crowmarsh is a suitable spot from which to observe activity. There are two runways, both 5,981ft in length: 01/19 runs roughly north/south and 06/24 runs roughly northeast/southwest.

Having opened in 1939 as a bomber airfield, Benson went on to find wartime fame through the exploits of its resident Spitfire and Mosquito squadrons which, under the operational control of Coastal Command, ranged far and wide over Europe bringing back photographic reconnaissance pictures of Bomber Command's piecemeal destruction of the Nazi war machine. Postwar, Benson maintained a heavy involvement in PR work with Mosquitoes, Lancasters, Canberras and Meteors until in 1953 the station was taken over by Transport Command and from 1961 until 1971 Argosies were a common sight here. The King's Flight re-formed here in 1946 and has remained at Benson ever since, latterly in the guise of the Queen's Flight.

The Queen's Flight currently operates Andover CC2 twin-turboprops, Wessex HC4 helicopters and the customised STOL jet BAe 146 CC2.

No 115 Squadron is also based here and operates Andover E3/3As for airfield calibration duties, but these do not constitute a high level of activity. At weekends, No 612 Volunteer Gliding School (VGS) accounts for most of the movements, currently with Grob G109 Vigilant T1s.

London and Oxford UASs and No 6 AEF are due to redeploy here in 1993 with the closure of Abingdon (qv).

Benson displays the arc of C-Type (Hipped) hangars typical of prewar Expansion Scheme airfield design. Behind them can be seen the technical site, airmens' accommodation and beyond that the station HQ buildings. *Andrew March*

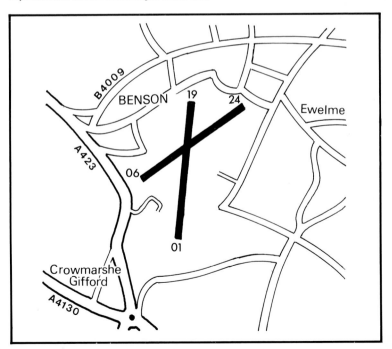

Bentwaters hosts two FS under the control of the 81st FW which operate the A-10A. Seen here at Bentwaters receiving attention from its groundcrew is an A-10A of the 510th FS. *John Dunnell*

Benson attracts an annual short deployment of US Air National Guard (ANG) C-130 Hercules transport aircraft, and other visitors somewhat intermittently. A plastic replica Spitfire is displayed by the main gate to mark Benson's wartime role with the type while a retired Andover serves the Fire Section for practice purposes on the airfield.

The best viewing can be had from a site by the A423 road between the runways at the west end; from the public minor road around the airfield on the north side near the threshold of runway 24; and from the minor roads leading south from Benson village which converge near the threshold of runway 06. Clearly, these had been the minor roads prior to the airfield's construction.

BENTWATERS

Suffolk (USAFE) EGVJ Tel: 0394 431861
OS Map Ref: TM34/53

This busy USAFE base is camouflaged into the Suffolk countryside between the A1152 to its north and the B1084 to its south, 12 miles east-northeast of Ipswich. There is only one runway, 07/25, which is 8,947ft long and follows a northeast/southwest axis. Bentwaters is due to close by mid-1993 and its future beyond that date is as yet uncertain.

Bentwaters opened in April 1944 under the control of Air Defence of Great Britain although it was not until December that its first fighter squadrons arrived, six of which operated Mustangs and Meteors from here at various times until September 1946. From then until August 1949 when it closed, Bentwaters was host to No 226 Operational Conversion Unit (OCU). The station remained on Care & Maintenance (C&M) until it was transferred to the USAF in March 1951. A

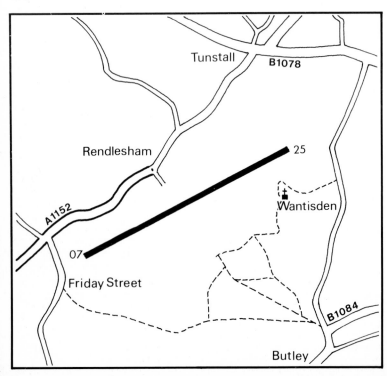

variety of aircraft types has served with the various resident USAF units in fighter and fighter-bomber roles: F-86 Sabre, F-84 Thunderstreak, F-101 Voodoo, F-4 Phantom, A-10 Thunderbolt and F-16 Fighting Falcon.

At the time of writing, Bentwaters is HQ of the 81st Fighter Wing (FW) which comprises four Fighter Squadrons (FS) each with 20 Fairchild A-10A Thunderbolt aircraft. The 92nd FS, with tailfin-tip yellow markings, and the 510th FS with purple, operate from here. The other two squadrons, the 78th and 91st, operate from RAF Woodbridge (qv) three miles to the south. All aircraft wear the two-letter base code 'WR' on their tail planes.

Bentwaters has regularly been the base for aircraft used in dissimilar air combat training (DACT), most recently with the General Dynamics F-16C Fighting Falcon aircraft. The former presence of based aircraft for this task certainly increased the number of visiting aircraft partaking in this training.

The main gate is reached from a roundabout on the A1152 road on the north side; it does not have a gate guardian. The operational area is on the south side of the runway with a separate security gate with access along tracks from Butley and Friday Street. The A-10A aircraft are allocated to scattered HAS, some sights of which can be obtained from a path around the perimeter fence on the south side. They operate in pairs and it is usual for two to taxi, take-off and land together which makes for interesting viewing and exciting photography. However, operations are normally confined to daytime on weekdays.

The favourite and best point for viewing, photography and parking is on the south side near the threshold of runway 25 at Wantisden Church, reached along a track from the minor road between Butley and Tunstall.

By mid-1993 the 81st FW will have retired its entire complement of A-10As, the best of its aircraft being allocated to the 92nd FS prior to the latter's removal to Spangdahlem, Germany, in early 1993 to form the first permanent Composite Wing in USAFE. This will enable Bentwaters to close completely.

BOSCOMBE DOWN

Wiltshire (MOD [PE]) EGDM Tel: 0980 623331 OS Map Ref: SU17/40

This enormous airfield is perched on top of a hill, two miles southeast of Amesbury. To its west, the A345 road follows the valley of the Wiltshire River Avon, and to its east the A338 follows the valley of the River Bourne. To its north, the A303 dual carriageway across Salisbury Plain is the only road to afford any distant sights of this airfield. There are two runways: the northeast/southwest 06/24 is 10,538ft long, and the south/north 17/35 is 6,918ft long.

Boscombe Down first opened in 1917 as a flying-boat training unit but had closed by the end of 1919. It was not until 1930 that Boscombe, by then rebuilt as a permanent station, re-opened as a home for the Virginias and Hinaidis of Nos 9 and 10 Squadrons. The station briefly came under the control of Coastal Command during 1937 but returned to Bomber Command in 1938. At the outbreak of war the station hosted Battles of Nos 88 and 218 Squadrons but they soon left for France and were replaced by the Aircraft & Armament Experimental Establishment (A&AEE) from Martlesham Heath. Throughout World War 2 the A&AEE carried out valuable work in testing new aircraft prototypes, in-service assessments of production aircraft, and weapons' trials. In May 1943 the Test Pilots' Training Flight was formed and renamed the Empire Test Pilots' School the following year before moving to Cranfield in 1945. Boscombe Down was also the home at various times to a number of other research and development units. Postwar, Boscombe Down has continued in its task of testing and trials, although the station itself has seen several major facelifts since the war.

Today, Boscombe Down is still the home of the A&AEE, and once again of the Empire Test Pilots' School (ETPS) and, as such is home to a small number of very varied types of aircraft, as large as a corporate BAC One-Eleven jet to as small as the latest single-engined turboprop Tucano trainer. The 'owned' aircraft are mostly painted in the attractive 'raspberry ripple' high-visibility red-blue colour scheme. The function of the A&AEE is still to test and prove new aircraft, new modifications, equipment and munitions for operational use; and the ETPS, the training of test pilots.

Aircraft from corresponding units of other

NATO members are among the visiting aircraft to this base. There are also occasional short deployments of USAF aircraft.

The Strike Attack Operational Evaluation Unit (SAOEU) with the latest Tornado F3 and Harrier GR7 aircraft, is also based here. By way of comparison, two replica SE5A biplanes, homebuilt and flown by members of the staff, are also based here.

The lie of the land does not make for easy viewing from any of the roads around the camp, but a reasonable view may be obtained from the embankments of the cuttings along the site of the former railway line between Grateley and Bulford Camp. The main gate, on the west side of the camp, is guarded by a pole-mounted Lightning in an attractive pose.

This base does not often open its doors to public inspection, but in 1990 the International Air Tattoo (IAT) staged the 50th Anniversary Battle of Britain Air Show here. The size of the camp and the length of the runways enabled large numbers of aircraft of all types and sizes to attend. This event proved very popular, such that in June 1992 it was the site for the Air Tournament International. It is hoped that use will be permitted of this site again.

In 1990 the International Air Tattoo (IAT) staged its 50th Anniversary of the Battle of Britain Air Show at Boscombe Down. *Brian Strickland*

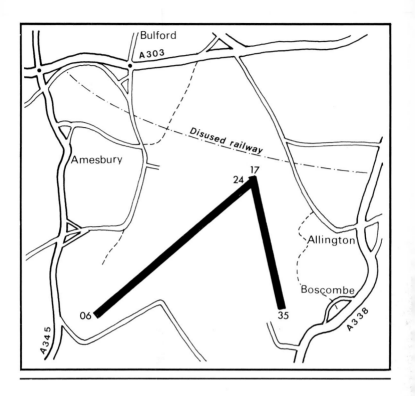

No 1 Tactical Weapons Unit at Brawdy operates some 36 Hawk T1A aircraft, exemplified here by XX247 of No 1 TWU/234 Squadron. *PRM*

BRAWDY

Dyfed (RAF) EGDA Tel: 0437 764571 OS
Map Ref: SM84/24

This RAF airfield is nine miles northwest of
Haverfordwest, north of the A487 coast road
to St David's Head, above the cliffs of St
Brides Bay, in southwest Wales. There are
two runways, north/south 02/20 7,369ft long,
and the southeast/northwest 15/33 6,006ft
in length.

Brawdy opened in February 1944 under
Coastal Command control and acted initially
as an alternative airfield for the Halifaxes of
Nos 58 and 502 Squadrons based at its par-
ent, St Davids. No 517 Squadron and its
Met Halifaxes was the first permanent resident at Brawdy from February 1944 until

September 1945. Immediately postwar,
Brawdy was the temporary home to detachments from No 595 Squadron (Spitfire) and
No 8 OTU (Spitfire and Mosquito). From
January 1946 until 1974 the station came
under control of the Fleet Air Arm (FAA),
with a number of Naval Air Squadrons operating from here. Brawdy returned to RAF
control in 1974 with the arrival of No 228
Operational Conversion Unit (OCU) and its
Hunters, soon to be re-designated No 1
Tactical Weapons Unit (TWU) in 1978. The
two component 'shadow' units — Nos 79
and 234 Squadrons — converted to Hawks
in 1984 and 1978 respectively.

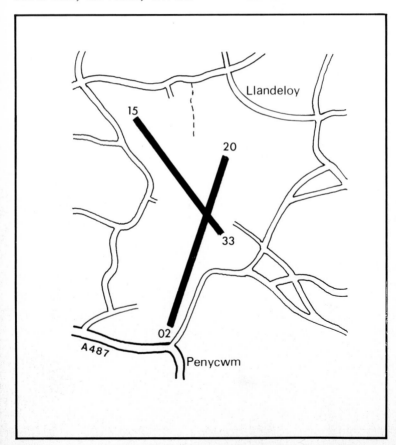

Located here, in the search-and-rescue (SAR) role, is B Flight of No 202 Squadron, with two Sea King HAR3 helicopters, providing cover for this large coastal sector of the UK.

Greatest activity is provided by No 1 TWU, to which is allocated approximately 36 Hawk T1A single-engined jet trainers, for use in the training of the tactical use of weapons. The aircraft are divided between Nos 79 and 234 Squadrons, the two 'shadow' squadrons.

The main gate is off a minor road that leads northwards from the A487 west of Penycwm, and some views of the aprons can be gained from further north along this road, but the hilly terrain generally makes this a difficult base to observe.

BRIZE NORTON

Oxfordshire (RAF) EGVN Tel: 0993 842551
OS Map Ref: SP29/07
The RAF's major air transport base in the UK is situated 14 miles west of Oxford, to the west of the A4095 and south of the A40(T) dual carriageway. The single runway 08/26 is some 10,007ft long. Brize Norton is a Military Emergency Diversion Aerodrome and operates 24hr a day.

Based here is the RAF's fleet of passenger airliner types with a worldwide deployment capability, many of which are easily converted to rapid passenger/freight configuration. No 10 Squadron operates the VC10 C1 passenger transport version, and No 216

Squadron the ex-British Airways and Pan Am TriStar 500s (C2); TriStar K1s, KC1s and K2 are capable of tanking duties.

No 101 Squadron is equipped with a fleet of nine ex-airliner converted VC10 K2/K3 inflight-refuelling tankers which, together with the TriStar KC1 and K2 aircraft with No 216 Squadron, comprise the Service's worldwide tanking capability.

When opened in August 1987, the Aircraft Engineering Squadron hangar in the northeast part of the site was the largest hangar in Europe, built to a unique cantilever design. This hangar is still used for maintenance.

Brize Norton is home to the RAF's VC10 fleet. No 10 Squadron operates the VC10 C1 passenger transport version, while No 101 Squadron flies the VC10 K2/K3 on air-to-air refuelling duties. *PRM*

The Air Movements School has some ground instructional airframes in its training hangar.

The minor road between Bampton and Brize Norton has traffic-light control for road traffic when aircraft are landing on the east/west 08/26 runway. The bridge over the disused railway line, on this road at the east end, affords a suitable spot from which to photograph these movements.

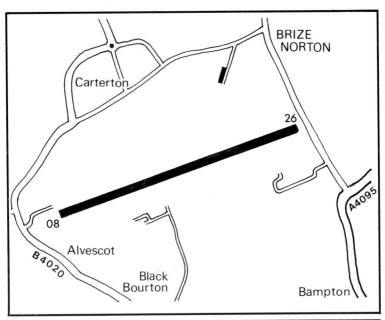

CHIVENOR

Devon (RAF) EGDC Tel: 0271 813662 OS Map Ref: SS50/34

RAF Chivenor is situated between the A361 and the north bank of the estuary of the River Taw, four miles west of Barnstaple. The main runway is 10/28 6,012ft long; the subsidiary runway 16/34 is 4,434ft long.

Chivenor opened in October 1940 as a Coastal Command airfield and its role until May 1942 was the operational training of Coastal Command aircrews with Blenheims, Ansons and Beauforts of Nos 3 and 5 OTUs. For the rest of the war Chivenor played a vital role in the Battle of the Atlantic with its Leigh Light-equipped Wellingtons flying countless anti-submarine patrols. Postwar Chivenor was transferred to Fighter Command in 1946, followed by a brief spell under Transport Command in 1950. No 229 OCU took up residence the same year with

Meteors and Vampires, converting in time to the Sabre and finally to the Hunter. The unit spent 24 years at Chivenor until it moved to Brawdy in 1974. The sole resident thereafter was No 22 Squadron and its Whirlwinds which had been providing an SAR capability since the late 1950s. In 1979-80 Chivenor was extensively rebuilt before No 2 TWU and its Hawks arrived in August 1980.

About 50 Hawk T1A jet trainers are based here with No 2 TWU which trains qualified pilots in the use of various munitions. The aircraft are divided between Nos 63 and 151 Squadrons, both of 'shadow' status, which would become autonomous units in a time of crisis. Aircraft allotted to No 151 Squadron wear a conspicuous single-letter code on the tailfin.

In the northwest corner of the site is the hangar used by A Flight of No 22 Squadron,

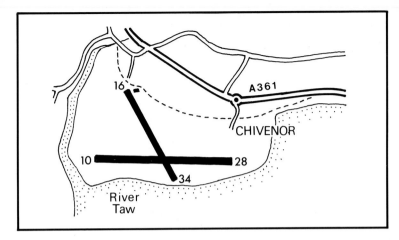

which operates two Wessex HC2 helicopters in the SAR role covering a wide section of the country's coast and shipping lanes.

At weekends, the powered Vigilant T1 gliders based here with No 624 Volunteer Gliding School (VGS) are usually the main source of activity.

This base is very active during the day on weekdays, and when runway 16/34 is in use

good photographs of the movements are possible from the northside footpath.

The former railway line between Barnstaple and Ilfracombe has been converted into a public footpath, along which seats have been provided. As this path runs parallel with much of the northern boundary of this airfield, it provides an excellent place from which to observe the aprons.

CHURCH FENTON

North Yorkshire (RAF) EGXG Tel: 0937 834666 OS Map Ref: SE52/37
Church Fenton is contained between the railway lines from Sheffield and Leeds to York to the west; the new route of the London-York line to the east; south of the B1223 Selby-Tadcaster road; and north of the B1222 between Sherburn and Cawood. It has two runways: 06/24 of 5,773ft in length, and 16/34 of 5,615ft.

Church Fenton opened in June 1937 as a fighter airfield and for the first two years of war it was a very busy place, some 11 squadrons seeing action from here with Blenheims, Hurricanes and Spitfires until the end of 1940. A short interlude as a fighter OTU airfield followed until, in May 1942, Church Fenton returned to frontline duties for the duration of hostilities in the day and nightfighter roles. Postwar, the station remained with Fighter Command, witnessing considerable activity with its resident Meteor, Hunter, Javelin, Mosquito and Hor-

net squadrons until it was transferred to Flying Training Command in 1959. Training of pilots on Jet Provosts by No 7 Flying Training School (FTS) continued until the station's closure in 1975. A pressing need to train more pilots soon became apparent and the station reopened in 1978 under RAF Support Command with No 7 FTS once more training pilots to fly, using Jet Provosts, a task it continues to this day.

No 7 FTS is now equipped with the Shorts Tucano T1 single-engined tandem-seat turboprop trainer, the first of the RAF's FTSs to convert to the type. On the tail of each aircraft, the base's identification letters 'CF' are intertwined and superimposed upon is the beak of a Toucan.

Two C-Type hangars and the aprons are north of runway 06/24, west of runway 16/34, and good views of the aprons can be had from the minor road between Church Fenton village and Ulleskelf along the western perimeter of the base. There is a dedi-

Hawk T1A XX202:P belongs to No 2 TWU/151 Squadron at Chivenor. *PRM*

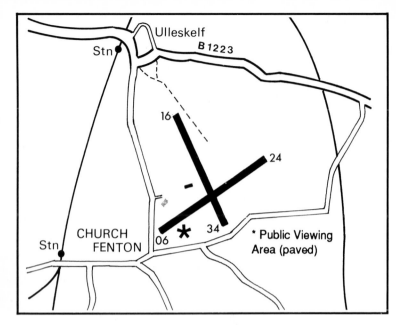

cated public viewing/parking enclosure by the southern perimeter of the airfield, west of the threshold of runway 34, on the north side of the minor road between Church Fenton village and Ryther.

The nearby former World War 2 bomber airfield at Elvington used to be a Relief Landing Ground (RLG). The station's Gate Guardian is a plastic replica Spitfire.

Church Fenton is once again doomed with closure, thanks to the Conservative Government's 'Options for Change' defence review of 1991, but there are plans for it to be retained as an ELG and as a RLG for Linton-on-Ouse.

Seen here on finals to land at Church Fenton is No 7 Flying Training School's (FTS) Tucano T1 ZF163. *PRM*

COLTISHALL

Norfolk (RAF) EGYC Tel: 0603 737361 OS Map Ref: TG25/23

RAF Coltishall is situated nine miles north of Norwich, west of the B1150 road. The main gate, hangars and aprons are to the west of the single runway 04/22, which is 7,500ft long.

Opened in June 1940 as a fighter station, Coltishall's wartime existence was immensely busy, playing host to a huge

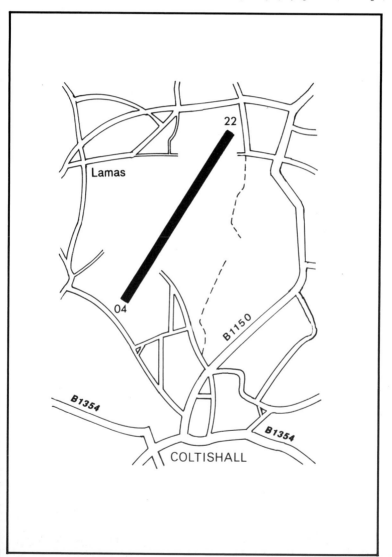

Type C hangars and a standard-pattern water-tower form a backdrop to two SEPECAT Jaguars at Coltishall. *Paul Jackson*

number of fighter squadrons and aircraft types engaged in day and nightfighting, antishipping patrols and intruder sorties. Amongst the aircraft types that operated from Coltishall at that time were Spitfires, Mosquitoes, Mustangs, Havocs, Beaufighters, Whirlwinds and Walruses. At the war's end, the station was no less busy, operating squadrons of Mosquitoes, Vampires, Meteors, Venoms and Javelins in the nightfighter role until in 1960 Coltishall became the first station to operate the all-weather EE Lightning fighter. A change of role followed when in August 1974 the strike-reconnaissance Jaguars of No 54 Squadron arrived, soon to be followed by those of Nos 6 and 41 Squadrons. Coltishall has also maintained an SAR presence since 1964, with No 22 and 202 Squadron's Whirlwinds, Wessex and Sea Kings. For a number of years the station was also host to the Battle of Britain Memorial Flight.

Three squadrons are currently based at Coltishall; Nos 6, 41 and 54, operating single-seat Jaguar GR1A tactical strike/reconnaissance aircraft, together with a handful of two-seat T2A models in the training role. The Jaguars operated by No 41 Squadron wear a single-letter tail code, while those of No 6 Squadron have a two-letter code commencing with the letter E, and No 54 Squadron with the letter G. These squadrons played a key role during Operation 'Desert Storm' in 1991 operating from forward bases in the Middle East

The SAR capability is maintained by No 202 Squadron's E Flight, operating Wessex HAR2 helicopters.

Extensions to the runway in past years have caused local roads to be severed, the remnants of which - particularly on the east side of the runway - afford quiet locations from which to observe and photograph the activities of this base. Additionally, views across the aprons can be had from the minor road on the northwest side of the base, although its position into the light makes it less suitable for photography.

CONINGSBY

Lincolnshire (RAF) EGXC Tel: 0526 42581; 0526 44041 (BBMF) OS Map Ref: TF22/57
This famous former World War 2 bomber airfield lies southeast of the A153 road, 12 miles northeast of Sleaford. It has one 9,000ft runway, 08/26.

Opened in 1940, Coningsby was one of the last of the prewar Expansion Scheme permanent airfields to be built and throughout World War 2 it operated as a heavy bomber airfield under No 5 Group Bomber Command. During the war years, six squadrons, including No 617 Squadron, operated from the station at different times with Hampdens, Manchesters and Lancasters, bombing European targets. Postwar, Coningsby remained under Bomber Command control, seeing a succession of Lincolns, Mosquitoes, B-29 Washingtons, Canberras and V-Force Vulcans until in 1964 the station was closed. It reopened in 1966 initially as a training station for Phantom air and ground crews, hosting No 228 OCU and No 5 School of Technical Training (SoTT), then as a frontline fighter base used in turn by Nos 6, 54, 41, 111 and 29 Squadrons. Coningsby became a Tornado base in 1987.

Today, Coningsby is home to four different Tornado F3 units: Nos 5 and 29 Squadrons are the two frontline units, the former's aircraft have two-letter tail codes, the first letter of which is A; the latter is similar, except that the first letter is B. No 229 OCU (shadow designation No 65 Squadron) is divided into Flights: A and B Flights handle conversion training and combat techniques, while C Flight is the standards section for instructor training. No 229 OCU's

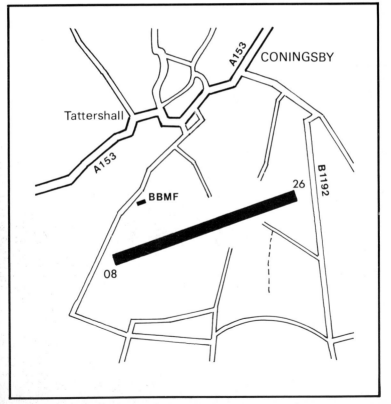

aircraft wear two-letter tail codes, the first letter of which is C. The Tornado F3 Operational Evaluation Unit (OEU) has some five Tornado F3 aircraft allocated for the testing of new equipment, but these do not carry identification codes.

No 29 Squadron is allocated to the HAS complex south of runway 08/26 at the western end, and No 5 Squadron to the HAS complex also south of the runway, but further east. No 229 OCU and the F3 OEU do not use HAS but use the hangars and aprons on the north side of the runway. Much of the activity here can be observed from the Battle of Britain Memorial Flight's Visitor Centre.

The Battle of Britain Memorial Flight (BBMF) has been based at Coningsby since 1976 and comprises one Lancaster, one Hurricane and five Spitfire aircraft, plus its own communications DH Devon and Chipmunk T10. The BBMF participates in scores of display events every year. The Flight's Visitor Centre is situated alongside the minor road south from Coningsby village and has its own car park. Tours of the Centre are conducted on weekdays, where heavy maintenance is carried out on the BBMF's aircraft, especially during the winter non-display period.

On the B1192 on the east side, and on the minor road on the west side, there are traffic lights to control road traffic when aircraft are taking off or on approach. These spots, and a number of former through roads around the base, afford good vantage points for photography.

During an exercise at Coningsby a Tornado F3 leaves a Phase 3 HAS. *Paul Jackson*

COTTESMORE

Leicestershire (RAF) EGXJ Tel: 0572 812241 OS Map Ref: SK91/14
This prominent airfield site is situated west of the A1(T), north of the B668, about nine miles northwest of Stamford. The road to the main gate, which is 'guarded' by a Can-

berra, leads from Cottesmore village. The single runway, 05/23, is 9,004ft long.

Opened in 1938 as an Expansion Scheme bomber station, after the outbreak of war Cottesmore played but a brief part as a bomber airfield in No 5 Group. The Hamp-

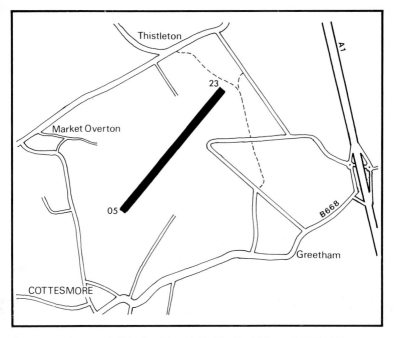

Cottesmore is home to the Trinational Tornado Training Establishment (TTTE) which operates the Tornado GR1/GR1T. Pictured is Tornado ZA548 bearing the fin-code B-10 which reveals it to be 'B' (British), and '10' (GR1T). *RAF*

dens of Nos 106 and 185 Squadrons were engaged in the early bomber offensive but by May 1940 the station had changed over to training bomber crews, a role it continued until mid-1943. Thereafter, the station came under USAAF control with troop carrier squadrons equipped with C-47 Skytrains and C-53 Skytroopers which played a part in Operations 'Overlord', 'Market Garden' and 'Varsity'. Postwar, the RAF resumed control and the station returned to a training role until, in 1954, it was transferred to Bomber Command once more. Cottesmore was redeveloped as a V-Bomber station and reopened in 1958 with Victors, later replaced by Vulcans. With the transferral of the nuclear deterrent to the Royal Navy, the V-Bomber squadrons left Cottesmore in 1969 and from then until 1980 the station was host to a range of different units equipped with ECM Canberras and Argosies, and Canberras of No 231 OCU. The year 1980 saw the arrival of the Trinational Tornado Training Establishment (TTTE), the station's current resident.

Today, Cottesmore is unique in the sense that it is the only UK air base to be the permanent residence of aircraft from a NATO ally other than the USA — the TTTE. The three nations involved are the UK, Germany and Italy, each operating Tornado IDS/GR1s. The Tornado OCU teaches selected pilots how to fly the aircraft. Luftwaffe aircraft have the shadow designation of JBG39.

TTTE aircraft wear fin codes with a prefix to denote the nationality (B-British, G-German and I-Italian) and a sequence of two-digit numbers of which 01 to 49 are applied to the dual-control GR1T (trainer) models, and 50 to 99 to the IDS/GR1 model. The aircraft themselves are operated on a pooled basis, with any permutation possible of the nationality of aircraft, pilot, navigator and instructor. The pooling arrangement means that the worn badges of A, B and C Conversion Squadrons and 'S' Standards Squadron (for instructor training) are of symbolic significance only.

The existence of aircraft on the visitors' ramp east of the runway at the south end near the main hangars can sometimes be established from the A1, but seldom their type(s) and never their identities. The minor roads between Thistleton, Market Overton and Cottesmore village on the north and west sides of the base, are too distant and too low to be of much help in this respect. The based operational aircraft line up on the south side of the runway, just west of the dog-leg bend in the minor road between Greetham and Thistleton. This is an excellent place, close to the taxiway, from which to view and photograph the aircraft.

The impressive main building of the RAF College, Cranwell, was designed by James West and opened in 1934 by HRH Edward, Prince of Wales. *MOD*

CRANWELL

Lincolnshire (RAF) EGYD Tel: 0400 61201
OS Map Ref: TM00/49

The prestigious Royal Air Force College, Cranwell, stands astride the B1429 road, north of the A17, four miles northwest of Sleaford, and between the A15 and A607, 12 miles south of Lincoln. The main runway, 09/27, is 6,831ft long and the subsidiary 01/19 is 4,803ft long.

Cranwell was originally opened in April 1916 as HMS *Daedalus*, an RNAS training establishment, and was taken over by the newly-formed RAF in April 1918 for officer cadet training. A new college building, designed by James West along the stylistic lines of the Royal Hospital, Chelsea, was officially opened by the Prince of Wales in October 1934. With the outbreak of war, Cranwell was tasked with the provision of advanced flying training of British and Commonwealth pupil pilots before their posting to OTUs. It maintained this very busy role throughout the war, eventually reverting to its primary task of officer cadet training in 1946. Several mergers and changes since the war have expanded the facilities of

Cranwell to include Departments of Specialist Ground Training, Air Warfare and Initial Officer Training, in addition to the flying training tasks undertaken by No 3 FTS.

Today, some 30 Tucano T1 turboprop trainers are used by No 3 FTS on Cranwell's main airfield, between the A17 and the B1429 roads, from both of which the day-time weekday movements can be observed and photographed. The aircraft have three-digit codes worn on the tail and nose. Visiting aircraft are rare. Nearby Barkston Heath with its 6,007ft runway 06/24 is used as a Relief Landing Ground (RLG), although at the time of writing it was closed to aircraft for major reconstruction work.

Static airframes for ground instruction are housed in the workshops on the eastern boundary of the main airfield.

The Cranwell Gliding Club of the RAF Gliding & Soaring Association (RAFGSA) is based on the Cranwell North airfield, to the north of the B1429 road. It has a single grass runway, 07/25, which is 3,690ft long. Gliding is normally undertaken here only at weekends during daylight hours.

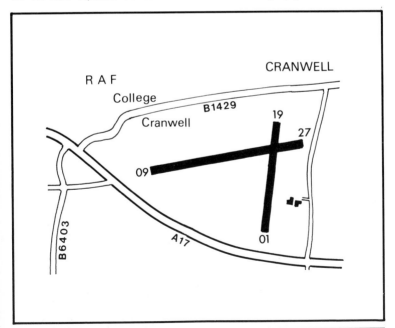

CULDROSE

Cornwall, HMS *Seahawk* (RN) EGDR Tel: 0326 574121 OS Map Ref: SW67/25

This Royal Naval Air Station (RNAS) is situated east of the A3083 road, immediately south of the town of Helston, on the road to Lizard Point. It has three runways: the main one, 12/30, is 6,006ft long, and the two subsidiaries are 07/25 (3,420ft), and 01/19 (3,455ft).

Opened in 1947, Culdrose was used initially as a Fleet nightfighter training station operating Fireflies and Hornets. During the 1950s it was host to a variety of different aircraft types, operated by a diversity of units, which included the AEW Skyraider and Gannet, and Sea Fury. As well as acting as a shore base for a number of disembarked frontline FAA squadrons, Culdrose became heavily involved with the training of Naval observers and latterly as the Royal Navy's premier helicopter training base, operating a wide variety of helicopter types since the late 1950s which have included the Hiller, Whirlwind, Dragonfly, Wessex and latterly the Sea King.

During the daytime on weekdays, Culdrose is alive with the swarms of helicopters belonging to the nine squadrons that are based here. Predannack with its two runways, further down the coast, is used as an RLG.

No 750 Squadron is the only fixed-wing operator on the station, using the Jetstream T2/T3 in the Observation and Communications aircrewman training role. No 705 Squadron operates some 20 Gazelle HT2 helicopters for pilot training and provides the machines for the RN's display team 'The Sharks'.

No 706 Squadron operates about 20 Sea King HAS5 helicopters in the anti-submarine warfare (ASW) training role. Nos 810, 814, 820 and 826 Squadrons are land-based here, but deploy operationally, with the Sea King HAS5 helicopter. No 849 Squadron is equipped with the electronic warfare version of the Sea King, the AEW2A, with which it also embarks operationally. No 771 Squadron is the SAR unit with about six Sea King HAR5 helicopters, and the RAF Sea

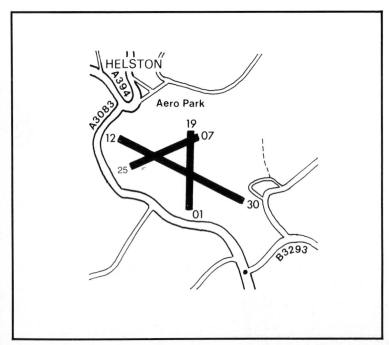

RNAS Culdrose hosts the RAF's Sea King Training Unit (SKTU) which operates a number of Sea King HAR3 helicopters, of which XZ587 is one, seen here overflying the base. *PRM*

No 750 Squadron is the only fixed-wing squadron at Culdrose and operates the BAe Jetstream T2/3. *Andrew March*

King Training Unit with a handful of Sea King HAR3s is also based here.

In addition to these operational aircraft, the School of Aircraft Handling has its own mobile ground instruction airframes, some of which can sometimes be seen from the perimeter.

The intense daytime flying activity often results in more than one runway being in use at any one time. During daylight hours at weekends the gliders of the Culdrose Gliding Club of the Royal Naval Gliding & Soaring Association may be seen operating from the field.

One good location with parking facilities from which to observe all the activity is the former Cornwall Aero Park, now a part of the Flambards Triple Theme Park, which is adjacent to the northside boundary fence. Alternatively, the layby off the B3293 road at the east end, north of the threshold to runway 30, affords views across the airfield.

FARNBOROUGH

Hampshire (MOD [PE]) EGLF (Civil) EGUF (Military) Tel: 0252 24461 OS Map Ref: SU86/54

Farnborough airfield is situated west of the A325 and north of the A323, about two miles from Junction 4 of the M3 motorway. It has three runways: the main, 07/25, is 7,874ft long; the two subsidiaries are 11/29 (4,494ft) and 18/36 (4,205ft).

Farnborough's history stretches right back to the dawn of manned flight when in 1905 the British Army's Balloon School was formed here. During World War 1 a number of RFC and RNAS aircraft, airship and balloon squadrons were stationed at Farnborough, together with the Royal Aircraft Factory. The latter was not only engaged in the design and construction of aircraft for the War Office, but also in research and development work (R&D). During the interwar period the R&D work at Farnborough assumed a growing importance although a number of RAF flying units also operated from here. With the outbreak of war in 1939, development work continued apace in such diverse areas as bomb-sights, camera

One of the highlights for the world aviation industry is the biennial SBAC Air Show at Farnborough held in September every other year. *PRM*

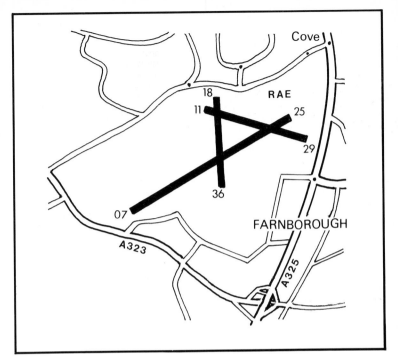

equipment and rocket projectiles, not to mention the evaluation of captured enemy aircraft. Post-World War 2, Farnborough has established itself as the world's foremost aerospace R&D institution and has gained added prestige through its hosting of the biennial 10-day SBAC Show, which concludes with a public air display on the final weekend.

Today, Farnborough is the oldest active airfield in the UK and the home of the Royal Aerospace Establishment (RAE) which operates more than a dozen different aircraft types for a wide range of test, develop-

ment and experimental purposes. Accident-damaged aircraft often arrive here for causal investigation by the Accident Investigation Bureau (AIB). The Institute of Aviation Medicine (IAM) is also based here, tasked with investigating the medical aspects of flying in relation to the human body.

Aircraft movements are not great and visiting aircraft few. The wooded perimeter to the south and west make for difficult viewing, but some movements can be seen from the minor road on the north side; park your car by the golf club.

FILTON

Avon (CIVIL) EGTG Tel: 0272 699094 (BAe) OS Map Ref: ST60/80
This large airfield is situated on the northern outskirts of Bristol, to the west of the A38 and east of the A4018, south from Junction 17 of the M5 motorway. Filton has two runways: 09/27 is 8,038ft long and 03/21 is 4,070ft long.

Filton can trace its origins as a site for aircraft manufacture back to 1910 when the British & Colonial Aeroplane Co Ltd was formed here. During World War 1 aircraft types like the Bristol Boxkite were built here and the RFC also used the airfield. The interwar period saw Filton playing host to No 501 Squadron AAF, No 2 ERFTS, as

Filton's aircraft manufacturing tradition goes back to World War 1. Today the British Aerospace factory is involved in F-111 maintenance for the USAF and conversion of VC10 aircraft for the RAF, in addition to the manufacture of components for the European Airbus programme. Here, British Airways' Airbus A320-111 G-BUSE forms a backdrop to one of Filton's earlier products, Bristol F2B Fighter D8096 (G-AEPH). *PRM*

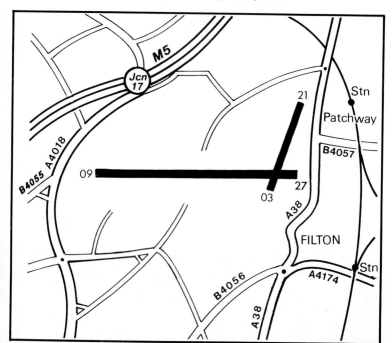

well as turning out such types as the Bristol Blenheim from its factory. With the outbreak of war, production of the Blenheim, Beaufighter and Beaufort was expanded and the airfield hosted a number of fighter units for the air defence of Bristol and its surrounding area. Postwar, the airfield and factories of Bristol, BAC, and its latest incarnation British Aerospace (BAe), have become famous for such high-profile projects as the ill-fated Bristol Brabazon and the world-famous BAC-Sud Concorde. Runway 09/27 was specially extended in 1946, at the expense of a whole village and several roads, to enable the huge Brabazon aircraft to take-off. Filton's involvement with civil aircraft manufacturing continues with the Airbus project. The Concorde flight simulator is also based here, used by British Airways for the training of its Concorde crews.

Having been the manufacturing base for military aircraft through two world wars, Filton's current military connection lies with the maintenance work undertaken on USAFE's F-111 fighter-bombers, and the conversion of ex-airline VC10 aircraft to the inflight refuelling role for the RAF.

On the south side of runway 09/27, Bulldog T1s of Bristol UAS and Chipmunk T10s of No 3 AEF can be found. These are most frequently operated at weekends. During the week, corporate aircraft belonging to BAe, Rolls-Royce and Turbo Union are active.

The A38 to the east is a busy road and offers no suitable places from which to observe aircraft movements. Neither do the roads which approach the factory from the south. The best viewing is from the stub of a once through-road on the north side of the runway, at about its mid-point, reached from a housing/trading estate on to an area of derelict land. However, as this faces the predominant light, it is not good for photography.

FINNINGLEY

South Yorkshire (RAF) EGXI Tel: 0302 770771 OS Map Ref: SK65/99
RAF Finningley lies between the A638 to the west and the A614 to the east, about six miles southeast of Doncaster, and to the south of the Doncaster-Gainsborough railway line. (Finningley railway station is only open for the annual air show.) There is one runway in use, 02/20, 9,004ft long.

Finningley opened in 1936 as a grass airfield in Bomber Command and up to the outbreak of war in 1939 it hosted several squadrons operating Wellesleys, Audaxes and Whitleys. For the first year of war the station trained bomber crews before it became involved briefly in the early bomber offensive with the Hampdens of resident No 106 Squadron. From March 1941 until the

A Hercules takes-off from Finningley with the village church in the background. *Paul Jackson*

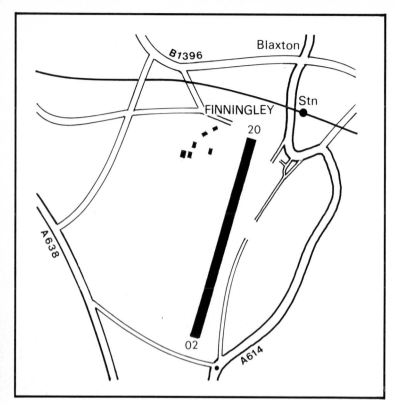

end of the war Finningley reverted to the operational training role with Nos 18 and 25 OTUs. Postwar, the station was transferred to Flying Training Command until its closure in the mid-1950s for conversion to a V-Bomber base. Finningley's new residents were Canberras, Valiants and Vulcans and they continued the station's association with Bomber Command and its successor Strike Command until 1970 when it was transferred to Training Command. The station continues to operate in the flying training role today.

Currently based here is No 6 FTS with a variety of aircraft types which include the twin-turboprop Jetstream T1 and the twin-turbojet Dominie T1.

Finningley is also home to the HQ of the RAF's SAR Wing which comprises No 22 Squadron operating four detached Flights of Wessex HC2 helicopters; and No 202

Squadron operating five detached Flights of Sea King HAR3 helicopters. The SAR Engineering Wing which maintains the helicopters of both squadrons is also based here.

Other units based here are the Yorkshire UAS with the Bulldog T1 and No 9 AEF with the Chipmunk T10

As a training base, most fixed-wing movements tend to be during daylight hours on weekdays, with the UAS and AEF flying at weekends. Viewing from the east side is excellent from the two no through-roads of what was originally the A614 (now diverted).

With so many aircraft of different types based here, the annual Battle of Britain air display in September has a good reputation for its exciting massed flypast, as well as attracting some interesting visiting aircraft to the event, so much so that there is invariably road traffic chaos!

HONINGTON

Suffolk (RAF) EGXH Tel: 0359 269561 OS Map Ref: TL89/74

This RAF airfield is situated between the A134 to the west and the A1088 to the east, about six miles south of Thetford. Honington's single runway, 09/27, is 9,012ft long.

Opened as a bomber station in May 1937 in No 3 Group, Wellington squadrons from Honington played a key role in the bomber offensive during the opening years of World War 2. In September 1942 the USAAF took over control of the station as a servicing

Honington is home to No 13 Squadron which is equipped with the reconnaissance variant of the Tornado, the GR1A. *Andrew March*

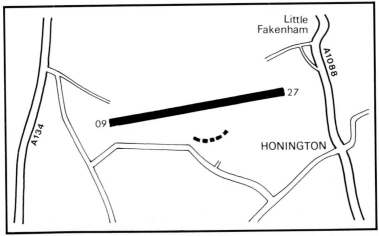

depot for B-17 Flying Fortresses. In February 1944 the 364th Fighter Group arrived with P-38 Lightnings for long-range bomber escort missions, converting later to the P-51 Mustang and remaining at Honington until November 1945. Postwar, Honington returned to RAF control as a bomber station, its Canberra Bomber Wing seeing action over Suez in 1956, while five squadrons of Valiants and Victors operated from here as part of the V-Force until 1966. The next phase in the station's life opened in 1969 with the arrival of the RAF's Buccaneer squadrons and an OCU, although their residency was eclipsed by the arrival in 1981 of the Tornado Weapons Conversion Unit (TWCU) with its Tornado GR1s.

Today, this station remains the busy home of the TWCU and of No 13 Squadron which operates the Tornado GR1A reconnaissance variant. The TWCU bore the shadow designation of No 45 Squadron until April 1992 when it became No 15 Squadron, following the disbandment of No 15 Squadron at Laarbruch, Germany. It has an operational commitment in wartime and a complement of some 20 Tornado IDS/GR1 aircraft to familiarise crews with the aircraft as a weapons system. The TWCU will redeploy to Lossiemouth (qv) from mid-1993.

The aircraft can be observed from the minor road, past the main gate, along the southside of the airfield; and from the no through-roads at the northeast and northwest corners. Jet efflux makes good photography a real challenge.

KINLOSS

Grampian (RAF) EGQK Tel: 0309 672161
OS Map Ref: NJ07/62
Guarding the northern tip of the UK, Kinloss is bordered by Findhorn Bay to the west and Burghead Bay to the north, and is on the southern shore of the Moray Firth. It is situated east of the B9011 Forres-Findhorn road, and north of the B9089 Forres-Burghead road. The one remaining operational runway, 08/26, is 7,582ft long.

Nimrod MR2 XV242 of the Kinloss Maritime Reconnaissance Wing overflies its Scottish base. *PRM*

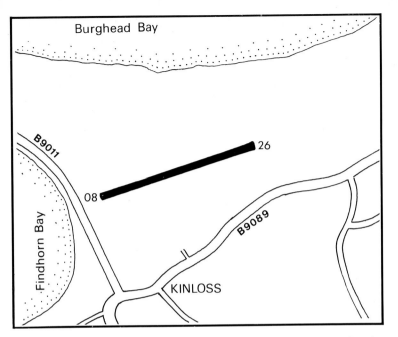

Burghead Bay

B9011

26

08

Findhorn Bay

B9089

KINLOSS

Kinloss opened in 1939 under the control of Bomber Command. Its resident unit for the duration of the war, No 19 OTU, used a variety of different marks of Whitley and Wellington in the training of heavy bomber crews. Postwar, the station passed to Coastal Command where No 236 OCU trained crews for Lancasters, Neptunes and Shackletons. Since 1949, Kinloss has been a maritime reconnaissance station: No 120 Squadron has operated from here continuously since then with Lancasters, Shackletons and latterly Nimrods; No 217 Squadron with Neptunes from 1952-57; Nos 201 and 206 Squadrons with Shackletons until 1965; and No 8 Squadron from 1972-73 with AEW Shackletons.

Currently based here are Nos 120, 201

and 206 Squadrons which together form the Kinloss Maritime Reconnaissance Wing operating the Nimrod MR2/2P aircraft. These aircraft are pooled but carry separate squadron badges although without distinctive code markings. No 236 OCU will redeploy to Kinloss from St Mawgan (qv) by the end of 1992, and all Nimrods will then be co-located here.

The Fulmar Gliding Club of the RAFGSA and No 663 VGS, the latter with Vigilant T1 powered gliders, operate from here at weekends, and sometimes on weekdays outside normal hours.

The main gate is on the B9089 and the hangars and aprons are between it and the runway. Good views can be had from the B9011 at the western end of the runway.

LAKENHEATH

Suffolk (USAFE) EGUL Tel: 0638 521861
OS Map Ref: TL73/80
The airfield is situated on the west side of the A1065, eight miles west of Thetford, and east of the B1112. An F-100D Super Sabre gate guardian is spectacularly mounted by

the main gate. There is a single runway, 06/24, 9,000ft long.

Lakenheath opened in 1941 although it was not until April 1942 that the RAF's No 149 Squadron and its Stirlings moved in, taking part in bombing, mining and resis-

Lakenheath has a large number of World War 2 Nissen huts which have been modernised and are still in use. In the foreground can be seen one of the newly-arrived F-15Es.
Paul Jackson

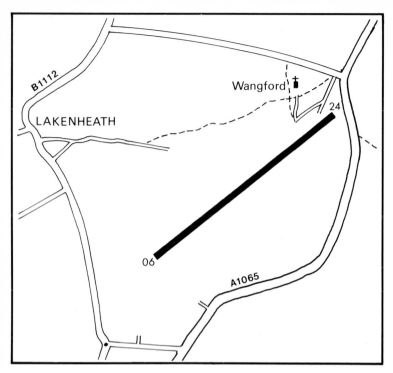

tance operations with No 3 Group Bomber Command until the squadron's departure in May 1944. Another Stirling squadron, No 199, arrived in June 1943 and stayed until May 1944. From mid-1944 the station was closed for major rebuilding, reopening in July 1948 under USAF control. A succession of Bomb Groups and Wings were stationed here over the next few years operating such aircraft types as the B-29 Superfortress, B-36 Convair and B-47 Stratojet in the bombing role; the RB-36, RB-50 and U-2 in the reconnaissance role; and in the refuelling role, the KB-29 and KC-97. In 1956 the USAF left Lakenheath and the base remained empty until early in 1960 when the 48th TFW arrived with the F-100D.

Today, Lakenheath is a major base of USAFE with the 48th FW still based here with about 80 F-111F fighter-bombers shared between the four component Fighter Squadrons (FS). The aircraft carry the base two-letter code LN on the tail, and colour banding on the top of the tail denotes to which squadron the aircraft is allocated, ie:

492nd FS blue, 493rd FS yellow, 494th FS red, and 495th FS green. F-111s of the 48th FW have played significant roles in both Operations 'El Dorado Canyon' in 1986 and 'Desert Storm' in 1991.

In 1992 the 48th FW has begun to exchange its F-111Fs for the F-15E Eagle. By the end of 1992 only two squadrons will be assigned to the 48th FW, the 495th FS and one other being deactivated.

Aircraft are housed in clusters of individual HAS on the south side of runway 06/24. This area can be seen from the verge of the A1065 road. Visiting aircraft tend to park in this area; identification of these is not always possible because of obstructions such as ground equipment and opened HAS doors. Occasionally, visiting C-130 Hercules or diverted aircraft from Mildenhall (qv) park on the north side of the runway.

The civilian Lakenheath Aero Club operates a small number of civil-registered aircraft from the base for Club members.

When runway 24 is in use, excellent photographic opportunities exist from a track on the east side of the A1065 near the approach lights, to capture aircraft on final approach. It is possible to park here, but take care not to block access to the Forestry Commission land. The road to the crash gate and to Wangford church in the northeast part of the site gives good views across the airfield, and especially of the spectacular groundshaking take-offs of F-111s with both afterburners lit.

It is possible to gain access to the high ground behind the control tower, both from a road leaving the B1112 next to a chip shop in Lakenheath village, and from a public footpath close to the northern boundary fence between Lakenheath village and Wangford church.

Periodically, Lakenheath will host an air show. In 1989 and 1990, in connection with Operation 'Excalibur', special arrangements were made to host photographers wishing to record the many aircraft visiting. On such occasions the base is especially worth a visit.

LEE-ON-SOLENT

Hampshire HMS *Daedalus* (RN) EGUS Tel: 0705 550143 OS Map Ref: SU55/01
This compact airfield is situated west of the B3385, on the north bank of the Solent, on which there is a hovercraft slipway, four miles west of Gosport. The main runway, 05/23, is 4,294ft long.

Opened in 1917 as a Naval seaplane training school, Lee-on-Solent was transferred to RAF control in 1918 and became the RAF Seaplane Training School in 1921. Its designation changed during the interwar period, but its task of training RAF and RN seaplane crews continued until the late 1930s when the station was also shared with a number of FAA squadrons and Coastal Command HQ. During the war years, Lee was used by a number of different FAA squadrons and units flying Fulmars, Ansons, Seafires, Sea Hurricanes and Barracudas. Joined by several RAF and US Navy fighter squadrons in 1944, the FAA's No 3 Fighter Wing was in action from Lee on D-Day and afterwards, although by the war's end it had returned to relative quiet. Postwar, the station played host to the usual disembarked frontline units together with a training and communications commitment. Its primary role in later years has been as the FAA's major technical training establishment, although a number of minor support units are in residence, such as the RN Accident Investigation Unit.

Lee's longest-serving unit was No 781

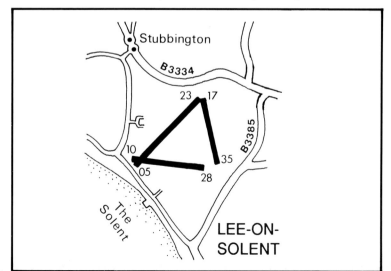

Squadron, formed in 1939 as a communications unit flying Walruses. It served at Lee until 1981 (with a disbandment between 1945-46), latterly in the SAR and communications roles with the Wessex 5, Heron and Devon.

Today, the RNAS at Lee-on-Solent is HQ of the Flag Officer NAS. Most of the based airframes are helicopters for ground use only with the Air Engineering School (AES). The Naval Hovercraft Trials Unit was based here for a time for mine countermeasures' trials.

Operational units are the Southampton UAS with the Bulldog T1 aircraft and the Portsmouth Naval Gliding Club of the RNGSA, which is usually active from here at weekends.

Visiting civil and military fixed-wing aircraft and helicopters tend to park in proximity to the control tower, which can be observed from Kingsmead Avenue or Glenthorne Close in the housing area to the west side of the base.

LEEMING

North Yorkshire (RAF) EGXE Tel: 0677 423041 OS Map Ref: SE31/88
Leeming is situated to the east of the A1(T) — due to be rebuilt to motorway standard — five miles southwest of Northallerton. There is one runway, 16/34, which is 7,520ft long.

Leeming opened in 1940 as a bomber airfield, one of the last prewar Expansion Scheme permanent stations to be completed. During the opening years of the war its resident Whitley squadrons played a leading role in the Battle of the Barges. As the war progressed, so too did Leeming's involvement in the strategic bomber offensive. Early in 1943, Leeming was trans-

ferred to the control of No 6 (RCAF) Group under whose command two Canadian Halifax squadrons flew intensive bomber operations against Axis targets until the end of the war. Postwar, the station was used for training fighter pilots, operational conversion training and latterly basic flying training. In the late 1980s the station closed for major runway extension work and a general rebuilding programme for the benefit of its current residents.

Today, Leeming is home to three squadrons of Tornado ADV/F3 aircraft. No 11 Squadron, using two-letter codes beginning with the letter D on the tail of its

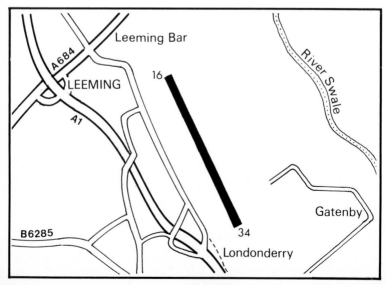

Leeming is host to three Tornado F3 squadrons. No 11 Squadron's aircraft sport two-letter tail codes commencing with 'D' as shown by ZE788. *Andrew March*

aircraft, operates from a large C Type hangar; No 23 Squadron, using two-letter codes commencing E, and No 25 Squadron with two-letter codes commencing F, operate from two new HAS complexes. The station is equipped with Quick Reaction Alert (QRA) Interceptor facilities to cover the Northern Q of the UK Air Defence Region (UKADR).

The Northumbrian UAS with the Bulldog T1 and No 11 AEF with the Chipmunk T10 are also based here. Dishforth with its two runways is used as an RLG.

The new main gate is on the minor road which was formerly the A1 through Leeming Bar, parallel with the present A1 dual carriageway. There is good parking and viewing available at the Londonderry Coach Park at the southern end of this section of road.

LEUCHARS

Fife (RAF) EGQL Tel: 0334 839471 OS Map Ref: NO45/20

Leuchars is situated on the east coast of Scotland, between the Firth of Forth and the Firth of Tay, seven miles south-southeast of Dundee, east of the A919. There are two runways: 09/27 is the main and 8,491ft long; 04/22, the subsidiary, is 4,803ft long.

Leuchars opened as an RNAS airfield in 1918 and during the ensuing years of the interwar period it acted as a shore base for a number of fleet fighter Flights and first-line squadrons. In 1938, Leuchars passed to

RAF Coastal Command under whose operational control it remained for the duration of World War 2, its various squadrons flying anti-submarine, anti-shipping and minelaying sorties with Beauforts, Beaufighters, Hudsons and Mosquitoes. From 1941, BOAC also operated a return service between Leuchars and Sweden using Mosquitoes to carry mail and return to the UK with high-grade engineering products, like ball-bearings, from Stockholm. The USAAF detachments also based here from mid-1944 flew secret missions using B-24

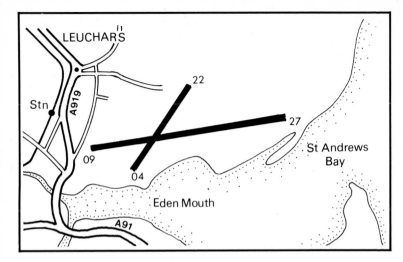

Liberators and C-47 Skytrains in support of the Norwegian underground movements, and to ferry passengers from Sweden to the UK. Postwar, Leuchars transferred to Fighter Command in 1950 and a succession of jet fighter types have operated from the base, including the Meteor, Vampire, Javelin, Hunter, Lightning and Phantom. An SAR facility has also been operated from here since 1954.

Today, Leuchars is a QRA station and a Military Emergency Diversion Aerodrome. Twenty-two new HAS have been built to accommodate the Tornado F3s of Nos 43 and 111 Squadrons, both of which recently converted from the Phantom FG1. No 228

OCU (shadow designation No 64 Squadron) and its Tornados are housed in the C Type hangars north of runway 09/27, west of the intersection.

One hangar is the province of B Flight No 22 Squadron which operates a detachment of Wessex HC2 helicopters in the SAR role.

Aberdeen, Dundee and St Andrew's UAS is also based here with five Bulldog T1 trainers.

The annual Battle of Britain/at Home Display is held in September and is another event with an excellent reputation for a good show with interesting visiting aircraft.

LINTON-ON-OUSE

North Yorkshire (RAF) EGXU Tel: 0347 4261 OS Map Ref: SE48/60
This airfield lies on the Ouse Plain, west of the A19 road, 10 miles northwest of York. There is a single runway, 04/22, which is 6,020ft long.

Linton-on-Ouse opened in 1937 as one of the earlier Expansion Scheme permanent bomber stations. It was not until the spring of 1940 that Linton's Whitleys were ready for operations. Plt Off Leonard Cheshire (later Gp Capt, VC) won an immediate DSO with No 102 Squadron during a raid on Cologne in November 1940, characterising the high profile that the station's aircrews

were to play in the strategic bomber offensive throughout World War 2. In mid-1943, the station was transferred to the control of No 6 (RCAF) Group and its squadrons operated Lancasters and Halifaxes until the end of the war. Postwar, Linton was transferred briefly to Transport Command before Fighter Command took over in mid-1946, with a number of squadrons flying Hornets, Meteors, Sabres and Hunters until the station's closure in 1957. It reopened later the same year as a Flying Training Command station engaged in basic flying training, a role it has maintained to this day under the auspices of RAF Support Command.

Today, No 1 FTS is based here with a fleet of Tucano T1 trainers. Most of the flying training is undertaken on weekdays only. Nearby Topcliffe with its two runways is used as an RLG, a role that is expected to be taken over by Church Fenton upon the demise of No 7 FTS there.

No 642 VGS operates from here at the weekends with Vigilant T1 powered gliders.

There is a viewing area set aside on the north side of the minor road between Aldwark Toll Bridge and Newton-on-Ouse/A19 to the east. This area is between the threshold of runway 04 and the main gate, guarded by a Jet Provost. Not only does it give a good view of the aprons outside the C Type hangars, but also a good opportunity to photograph the aircraft taxiing and taking off.

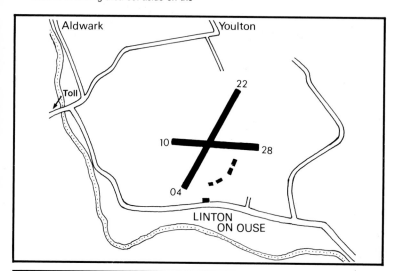

LOSSIEMOUTH

Grampian (RAF) EGQS Tel: 0343 812121
OS Map Ref: NJ21/70

Lossiemouth is situated close to the south shore of the Moray Firth, four miles north of Elgin, west of the B9135 and south of the B9040. It has two runways: the main is 05/23, which is 9,091ft long; the subsidiary, 10/28, is 6,590ft long.

Opened in 1939 as a permanent station, for the duration of World War 2 No 20 OTU at Lossiemouth trained bomber crews. A maintenance unit also shared the airfield. On 12 November 1944, Lancaster bombers of Nos 9 and 617 Squadrons arrived with special Tallboy bombs and used Lossiemouth as a forward base from which they successfully attacked and capsized the German battleship *Tirpitz* in Tromsö Fjord, Norway. Postwar, Lossiemouth was taken over by the Royal Navy, named HMS *Ful-mar*, and continued in the training and maintenance role until it was returned to RAF control in 1972. The first RAF unit to take up residence was No 8 Squadron and its Shackleton AEW2s, followed by Jaguars of Nos 6 and 54 Squadrons, and No 226 OCU.

Today, Lossiemouth is an exceedingly active base hosting five different units operating four different types of aircraft of various marks. No 226 OCU with the Jaguar GR1A, T2 and T2A, for the flying conversion to type of pilots, is based on the northside of the base, west of the threshold of runway 23. It bears the 'shadow' designation of No 16 Squadron.

No 237 OCU, with similar duties, has both the Buccaneer S2B, and the Hunter T7 and T8C types based in the C-Type hangars between the two runways in the northeastern part of the base.

A mixture of hangars can be seen at Lossiemouth. These include a Type C (12 bay) and Type J (curved roof). Also visible are two of the station's Buccaneers and a Falcon 20.
Paul Jackson

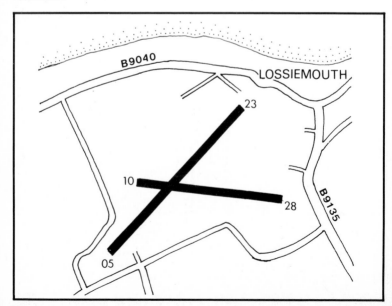

No 12 Squadron, in the Anti Surface Warfare (ASUW) role, operates the Buccaneer S2B and the Hunter T7, T7A and T7B from the HAS complex in the northwestern part of the base. The squadron is due to disband by April 1993 and will be replaced by No 27 Squadron and the Tornado GR1 from Marham (qv), No 27 being renumbered as No 12 Squadron.

No 208 Squadron, also in the ASUW role, operates the Buccaneer S2B and the Hunter T7 and T7B from the HAS complex on the south side of the base, south of the intersection of the two runways. The squadron is due to disband in October 1993, its role being taken over by the Tornado GR1s of No 617 Squadron from Marham.

The SAR/Mountain Rescue facility for this area is covered by D Flight of No 202 Squadron which has two Sea King HAR3 helicopters and is also deployed on the southside of the base. There is a Mountain Rescue Post just west of the base.

Views on to the base are generally good from all the perimeter roads, and photographic opportunities are especially propitious from the golf course near to the threshold of runway 23.

LYNEHAM

Wiltshire (RAF) EGDL Tel: 0249 890381 OS Map Ref: SU02/78

Lyneham is situated on top of a hill, south of the M4 motorway between Junctions 17 and 16, west of the A3102 Calne-Swindon road, and south of the B4069 (formerly the A420) Lyneham-Chippenham road. It has two runways: the main, 07/25, is 7,830ft long; the subsidiary, 18/36, is 5,991ft long.

Opened in 1940, Lyneham's contribution to the war effort included the provision of basic flying training and No 301 Ferry Training Unit for overseas delivery of aircraft from the station's No 33 Maintenance Unit (MU). Courier and VIP services were operated by Liberators, Dakotas and Yorks of No 1425 Flt, and latterly by No 511 Squadron. The station's involvement in air transport duties continued after the war with Stirlings, Yorks and Hastings flying worldwide routes for the RAF. No 216 Squadron at Lyneham became the world's first military jet transport squadron in 1956 when it re-equipped with the DH Comet C2. Bristol Britannias arrived

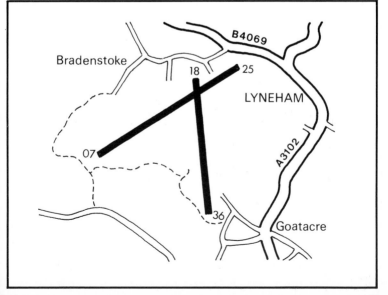

in 1959 and both types served alongside each other in the aero-medical and strategic transport role until No 511 Squadron moved to Brize Norton (qv) in 1970 and No 216 Squadron disbanded in 1975. The first Lockheed C-130 Hercules arrived at Lyneham in 1967 and at its peak the Lyneham Wing comprised six Hercules squadrons. During 1990, Lyneham's Hercules fleet celebrated its one-millionth flying hour.

Today, the RAF's tactical transport fleet of some 40 C-130 Hercules aircraft is based here with Nos 24, 30, 47 and 70 Squadrons, and No 242 OCU. The aircraft do not wear distinctive unit markings and are collectively pooled under the Lyneham Transport Wing. The aircraft, be they Mk 1 or Mk 3 variants, are probe-fitted for inflight refuelling, and a small number are the dedicated C1K tanker model conversion. These aircraft deploy to equip No 1312 Flt at Mount Pleasant airfield in the Falkland Islands. Lyneham and its Transport Wing provided crucial logistical support to British Forces in the Gulf during Operation 'Desert Storm' and in the postwar supply drops to Kurdish refugees in northern Iraq and Turkey during 1991.

Most of Lyneham's visiting aircraft are of like type and function, from a variety of nations. These relatively large aircraft occupy the wide aprons to the east of runway 18/36. Views across the base can be had from the tracks to the perimeter fence from Bradenstoke village off the B4069; from the B4069 near the threshold of runway 25; from the A3102 south of the main gate; and from the minor road from Goatacre to New Zealand. From here there is a bridleway which passes round the end of runway 36 which is an excellent location for action photography. Another bridleway joins this via Catcomb Wood and Melsome Wood to Bradenstoke Abbey, passing around the threshold of runway 07 in the process.

Lyneham is home to the RAF's Hercules Transport Wing where Hercules C1P XV292 is pictured taxying, bedecked in special markings to celebrate the type's 25th year in RAF service. *PRM*

MARHAM

Norfolk (RAF) EGYM Tel: 0760 337261 OS
Map Ref: TF72/09

Marham is situated on the north side of the
A1122 between Downham Market and
Swaffham, 10 miles southeast of Kings
Lynn. There are two runways: the main,
06/24, is 9,140ft long; the subsidiary, 01/19,
is 5,900ft long.

Opened in 1915 as an RNAS, Marham
was originally known as Narborough. The
airfield was extensively rebuilt in the mid-
1930s as a part of the RAF's Expansion
Scheme, reopening in April 1937 as a heavy
bomber station. During the first few years of
war No 3 Group Wellingtons and Stirlings
from Marham played their part in the strategic bomber offensive. As the war progressed the station came successively
under the command of Nos 2 and 8 Groups,
its squadrons flying Mosquitoes in the night
bombing and pathfinding roles. In April
1944, Marham was closed for extensive runway reconstruction to take place, bringing it
up to Very Heavy Bomber standard.
Reopening in 1949, the following year saw
the B-29 Washington Conversion Unit set
up at Marham to train crews for the RAF's
heavy bomber squadrons. The mid-1950s
witnessed the formation here of a Canberra
Bomber Wing and in 1956 a new era in RAF
strike power dawned with the advent of the
V-Force, using Blue Steel-equipped
Valiants and Victors. Eventually the two
types were relegated to tanking duties when
the Vulcan superseded them in the nuclear
strike role. From 1977 until 1982, Marham
was home to Canberras of No 100
Squadron and No 231 OCU. However, the
base has maintained its links with the Victor
to this day; two of its squadrons - Nos 55

No 2 Squadron and its Tornado GR1As redeployed to Marham from Laarbruch in December
1991. By 1993 both the RAF's squadrons of reconnaissance Tornados will be based here.
Andrew March

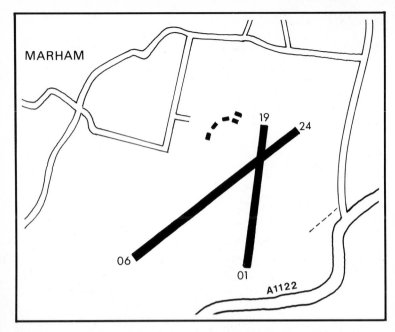

MARHAM

and 57 - played vital air-to-air refuelling roles in the Falklands campaign of 1982, and Operation 'Desert Storm' in 1991.

The sole surviving Victor squadron still based at Marham is No 55 with some 12 Victor K2 tanker aircraft which can usually be found on the aprons around the arc of C-Type hangars in the northwest part of the base. These are the last remaining Victors in service and are likely to be superseded in due course by the conversion to the tanking role of ex-airline VC10s. Although No 55 Squadron will disband by the end of 1993, the RAF's air-to-air refuelling capability will continue to be provided by Brize Norton's (qv) VC10 and TriStar aircraft.

Tornado IDS/GR1 and GR1T aircraft have been based here since 1983 with Nos 27 and 617 Squadrons. Their aircraft are allocated to the HAS complex to the east of runway 24, near to the threshold. Both squadrons played leading roles in the precision bombing of Iraqi targets during Operation 'Desert Storm' in early 1991, operating from forward bases in the Gulf. From April 1993, No 27 Squadron will redeploy to Lossiemouth (qv) and renumber to become No 12 Squadron in the Anti-Surface

Warfare (ASUW) role when No 12 Squadron and its Buccaneers disbands. No 17 Squadron will follow in October 1993 but will retain its identity when it takes over the ASUW role from No 208 Squadron and its Buccaneers when the latter also disbands.

No 2 Squadron with the Tornado GR1A redeployed from Laarbruch, Germany, to Marham in December 1991. No 13 Squadron, also equipped with the Tornado GR1A, will redeploy to Marham from Honington (qv) by August 1993, concentrating both of the RAF's Tornado reconnaissance squadrons at the one base.

The Groundcrew Reconnaissance Training Facility and Tornado Electronic Warfare Maintenance School will transfer here from Honington in mid-1993.

The Fenlands Gliding Club of the RAFGSA houses a variety of civil-registered gliders in one of the C-Type hangars. These are frequently flown at weekends.

Marham's perimeter road affords some good viewing locations, if somewhat distant, but photography of landings on runway 24 is good from the minor road to the east which aircraft overfly low before touchdown.

MIDDLE WALLOP

Hampshire (ARMY) EGVP Tel: 0264 384421 (Museum); 0264 38 plus the four-digit extension number, or Bulford Military Telephone Exchange 0980 33371 (Camp) and ask for who you want. OS Map Ref: SU30/39

This grass airfield is situated to the east of the A343, 12 miles northeast of Salisbury. Its single runway, 08/26, is grass, and just 2,400ft long.

Built as a prewar Expansion Scheme station, Middle Wallop opened in 1940 under the control of Fighter Command. During the Battle of Britain, Spitfires and Blenheims operated in the dayfighter role but by the end of 1940 No 604 Squadron, resident since July, converted to Beaufighters and the nightfighter role. It remained at Middle Wallop until December 1942. A number of fighter squadrons flew bomber escort and 'Rhubarb' sorties from the station in the following year, although by August the RAF had left Middle Wallop, replaced by ele-ments of the USAAF's IXth Fighter Command, involved in photo-reconnaissance duties with Spitfires and Mustangs. The station returned briefly to RAF Fighter Command control from July 1944 until early in 1945 when the Royal Navy took over Middle Wallop, naming it HMS *Flycatcher*. Return-ing to RAF control once again in April 1946 as a fighter station, it became increasingly involved with Army flying and in 1958 the station was formally transferred to the Army, becoming the Army Air Corps (AAC) Centre.

Today, Middle Wallop is principal airfield for the AAC, with very intensive circuit and instrument flying training by rotary and fixed-wing aircraft, both by day and night. Andover is used as an RLG.

The Basic Fixed-Wing Flight (BFWF) and the Forward Air Control Flight (FACF) oper-ate between them over 20 Chipmunk T10 aircraft. No 670 Squadron is equipped with about 30 Gazelle AH1 helicopters bearing large codes in Dayglo on the tail surfaces.

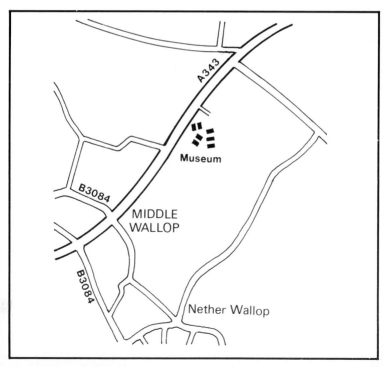

No 671 Squadron operates the Lynx AH1 and AH7 helicopters. Another interesting unit based here is the AAC Historic Aircraft Flight, operating examples of several aircraft types no longer operational with the AAC. These aircraft travel to many parts of the UK to participate at air shows during the display season. All units are housed in the large hangar complex in the northwest part of the base.

The School of Aeronautical Engineering (SAE), formerly the AETW, bases its collection of ground instructional airframes in Stockwell Hall. A further collection of grounded airframes and artefacts is kept and displayed in the Museum of Army Flying, housed in a new structure, adjacent to the A343, which has a car park. The Museum's cafeteria at first-floor level affords good views across the grass aprons and runways when the Gazelles are darting about.

A popular feature of the annual Army Air Day is the massed helicopter lift-off from the far side of the field, where they are temporarily obscured by the lie of the land, and the ensuing massed attack by literally dozens of these helicopters. Parascending takes place from here at weekends and on Public Holidays.

MILDENHALL

Suffolk (USAFE) EGUN Tel: 0638 512251/3
Mildenhall lies along the south side of the A1101, 12 miles northwest of Bury St Edmunds. It has a single runway, 11/29, which is 9,240ft long.

Opened in 1934, Mildenhall witnessed the historic MacRobertson England-Australia Air Race that same year which Charles W. A. Scott won in a de Havilland Comet racer. Prewar, the station hosted a number of bomber squadrons and with the outbreak of war Mildenhall was launched into the bomber offensive against Germany, a role in which the station and its resident squadrons would continue until the end of the war in 1945. Seven bomber squadrons operated from Mildenhall during the war years, flying Wellingtons, Stirlings and Lancasters. Postwar, the station remained under RAF Bomber Command control host-

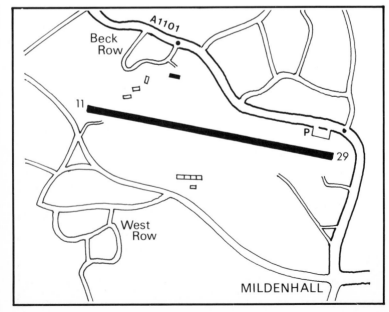

Mildenhall's annual air display which is held each May attracts a large number of visiting aircraft. *PRM*

ing at various times six squadrons operating Lancasters and Lincolns until, in 1950, it was transferred to the USAF. Under the control of Strategic Air Command (SAC), Bomb Wings rotated on Temporary Duty stays flying B-47s and B-50s. In recent years, Mildenhall has been involved in tactical airlift, air-to-air refuelling, airborne command & control, and strategic reconnaissance duties using a variety of aircraft types which have included the C-124 Globemaster, C-133 Cargomaster, C-130 Hercules, C-141 StarLifter and the enormous C-5 Galaxy transports; the KC-97, KC-10 and KC-135 tankers; the EC-135 and E-3A AWACS; and the breathtaking Mach 3 SR-71 Blackbird.

Today, Mildenhall is a major tactical staging post to Europe for US forces and is operated by USAFE. It is open seven days a week but is normally shut voluntarily for about six hours every night as part of a 'good neighbour' policy. However, when events in the Gulf took a turn for the worse during the autumn of 1990, US forces were rapidly deployed via Mildenhall together with tonnes of equipment, and showed how eas-

ily this policy could be waived in an emergency.

Currently, there are only three aircraft allocated to units based here: three UC-12M Beech Super King Airs of the US Navy, coded 8G (indicating the Naval Air Facility, Mildenhall) which are housed near the security gate on the southside. However, from mid-1992, Worldwide Airborne Command Posts have been centred at Offut AFB, Nebraska, within the 55th SRW, and detached overseas as necessary. Mildenhall is now one of the overseas bases that host EC-135s on a rotational basis.

The based 313th Tactical Airlift Group is responsible for the two-month long deployments of up to 16 C-130E/H Hercules aircraft from either the 314th Airlift Wing (ALW), 317th ALW or 463rd ALW from the continental USA. Similarly, the based 306th Strategic Wing controls the KC-135A, E, Q, and R Stratotankers and the KC-10A Extenders which pass through, or temporarily operate from, here.

In addition to these, the largest aircraft types to regularly visit Mildenhall are the C-141B StarLifter and C-5A/B Galaxy strategic transports of Military Airlift Command (MAC). The passenger terminal here is used as a gateway to Europe and in addition to these purely military aircraft types there are frequent movements of some of the larger civil airliners leased by, or operated on behalf of, the military authorities.

Thus, the interest generated by this base is great, to the extent that some local farmers have fields set aside specially for air-minded campers. There is a segregated sur-faced parking area by the A1101 road on the north side of the runway at the east end, and the roads each side of the runway offer good views. Aircraft tucked in by the control tower and in the terminal area can some-times be identified from the private garages of Tithe Avenue, south from the A1101 on the north side of the base.

Runway 29 is usually in use and good photographs of aircraft on final approach over the A1101 can be taken from the industrial estate south of the runway at the east end, and from the crash gate at the end of Folly Lane in this vicinity. When runway 06 is in use at Lakenheath, aircraft on approach to there overfly the west end of Mildenhall at a relatively low altitude. A pop-ular event is the annual Mildenhall Air Dis-play which is held in May.

NETHERAVON

Wiltshire (ARMY) EGDN Tel: 0980 33371
OS Map Ref: SU15/48
The AAC base at Netheravon is situated on the high ground of Salisbury Plain, above and east of the A345 road, 12 miles north of Salisbury. It has two grass runways: 11/29 is 3,582ft long, and 05/23 is 2,100ft long.

Netheravon can trace its origins back to 1912 although it was not until 1913 that the first two RFC squadrons moved in. Through-out World War 1 the station fulfilled a train-ing role, flying a variety of aircraft types which included the Avro 504. During the interwar period it continued in the training role, this time for Fleet Air Arm pilots. This affiliation with the Royal Navy continued until, in 1942, Netheravon became involved with the activities of the newly-formed No 38

A Lynx is caught flying in front of a Type A hangar at Netheravon. *Paul Jackson*

(Airborne) Group. Then began the training of RAF aircrews to tow Horsa gliders with Whitleys and Stirlings in preparation for Operation 'Overlord'. No 38 Group HQ left Netheravon in October 1944 and the station reverted to glider trials and pannier test-drops by Dakota and Halifax aircraft, along with the preparation of gliders for Operation 'Varsity' in March 1945. Postwar, Netheravon continued to train glider pilots and despatchers until, in 1948, all flying ceased. The RAF Police made the station its HQ from 1950-62 and in 1966 HQ Army Aviation Strategic Command assumed control of the whole station.

Today, No 656 Squadron is based here with six Lynx AH1 and six Gazelle AH1 helicopters, in support of 1st Infantry Division of UK Mobile Force. Also based here are No 658 Squadron with the Gazelle AH1 and Scout AH1 helicopters; No 666 (TA) Squadron with Scout AH1s; and No 2 Flight with Gazelle AH1s for liaison duties. The Army Parachute Association is also based here.

The location of this field makes observation difficult; the two grass runways are south of the three separate hangars which themselves are atop an escarpment. The best views are obtained at a distance from the minor road between Fittleton and Everleigh.

The main gate, on a tortuous minor road between Upavon and Bulford, acquired a Sioux AH1 as a 'guardian' during 1989.

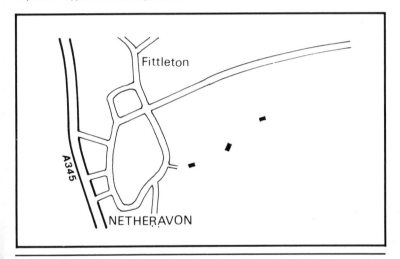

NORTHOLT

Greater London (RAF) EGWU Tel: 081 845 2300 OS Map Ref: TQ09/84
This famous former fighter base and former London Airport is on the north side of the A40 dual carriageway, three miles east of the eastern end of the M40 motorway, and west of London. The nearest London Underground tube station is Ruislip Gardens. It has one runway, 07/25, which is 5,525ft long.

Northolt opened in 1915 as a fighter station, although for much of World War 1 its primary role was in the training of pilots for night flying. With the end of the war, flying training ceased and during the interwar period Northolt witnessed the formation of Nos 600 and 601 Squadrons AAF, the London UAS and the arrival of a number of RAF fighter squadrons. In 1936 Northolt was transferred to Fighter Command and in 1938 the first RAF Squadron to receive the Hawker Hurricane was No 111 at Northolt. During World War 2, the station achieved lasting fame as a very active fighter base, seeing some 45 separate fighter squadron movements between 1939-44. From 1943

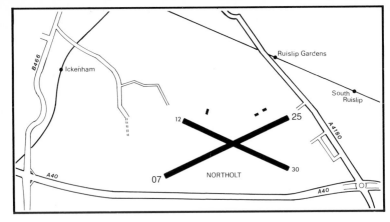

onwards, transport aircraft made increasing use of the station until, by 1946, Northolt became the main London Airport. In 1957 RAF Transport Command assumed control, and to this day Northolt maintains an important role as London's military airfield engaged in the transportation of VIPs and senior officers.

The main gate, complete with a plastic replica Spitfire, is on the east side of the camp, with access westwards from the A4180 — the former gate and layby on the north side of the A40 have both been closed because of extensive new roadworks and motorway extension.

The motorist can discern the airfield's

Northolt from the cockpit: Hercules C3P XV299 drifts over the A40 road below on finals to runway 07. *Jonathan Falconer*

presence from the miniature street lights where air traffic approaching runway 07/25 might be in peril of losing its landing gear.

No 32 Squadron is based in the hangars on the northern side of the base, with a variety of jet, propeller-driven and rotary aircraft, for VIP and communications duties. The squadron's aircraft and aircrew establishment has recently been augmented by the disbandment of No 60 Squadron at Wildenrath, Germany.

At times of Royal and overseas Head of State visits, governmental conferences, etc, VIP aircraft of other nations frequently visit here. Routinely, communications aircraft of NATO countries are frequent visitors, and use the parking aprons near to the former main gate on the south side of the base.

It is possible to view the airfield from Wingfield Way, off the A4180 to the east of the base.

ODIHAM

Hampshire (RAF) EGVO Tel: 0256 702134
OS Map Ref: SU73/49
This airfield is east of the A32, three miles south of Junction 5 on the M3 motorway. It has one runway, 10/28, which is 6,027ft in length.

Odiham opened late in 1936 as a permanent station in the Army Co-operation role, with a succession of resident squadrons operating the Lysander, Blenheim, Mustang and Tomahawk in this role until, in mid-1943, they became more involved with tacti-

cal reconnaissance and night intruder operations over occupied Europe. After D-Day, the station's resident squadrons flew PR sorties with Spitfires and Mosquitoes. A further change of role soon came with the arrival of Nos 264 and 604 Squadrons and their nightfighting Mosquitoes for a short stay at the end of 1944. At the end of the war Odiham was transferred to Transport Command, then Fighter Command, with a brief transferral to the RCAF during late 1945-46. Odiham hosted a number of RAF

No 7 Squadron's Chinook HC1 ZA707:EV, still in its 'Desert Storm' camouflage scheme, shows off its rear loading ramp at Odiham. *PRM*

fighter squadrons postwar operating the Tempest, Spitfire, Vampire, Meteor and Javelin, until Transport Command took over again in 1960. Then began the station's affiliation with helicopters, a link it has maintained to this day.

Currently No 240 OCU is based here with both the Puma HC1 and the heavylift Chinook HC1 helicopters. Also based here operationally is No 33 Squadron with the Puma HC1 and No 7 Squadron with the Chinook HC1.

The Kestrel Gliding Club of the Army Gliding Association is based in a hangar at the southeast corner of the base and usually operates only at weekends. During the summer months, gliding often takes place on Monday, Tuesday and Friday from 1700hrs until dusk.

The surrounding geographical contours make this airfield difficult to observe, but distant views of the aprons can be obtained from the minor road between the A32 and Long Sutton, to the south of the base. Normal operations are during the daytime only, on weekdays.

The close proximity of Farnborough (qv) makes Odiham a popular airfield for visiting aircraft when the biennial SBAC Air Show is taking place. Infrequent deployment of USAF C-130 Hercules aircraft also occur.

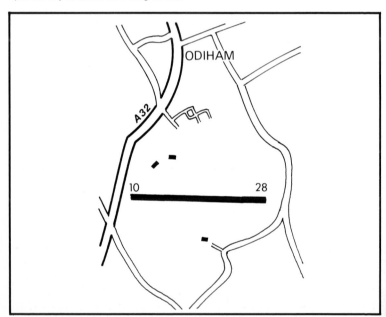

PORTLAND

Dorset HMS *Osprey* (RN) EGDP Tel: 0305 820311 OS Map Ref: SY68/74
This RNAS covers only a small physical area to the east of the A354 road, at the north end of the Isle of Portland, on the southern shore of Portland Harbour with which there is a hovercraft slipway connection. A very short runway, 04/22, of 750ft in length, supplements a collection of helipads.

Portland opened in 1917 as the shore establishment HMS *Sereptia* under control of the RNAS, with floatplanes using the harbour from which to mount anti-submarine patrols. The station fell briefly under RAF control at the end of World War 1 although it was not until 1939 that any significant involvement with aircraft occurred when No 772 Squadron formed, flying the Fairey

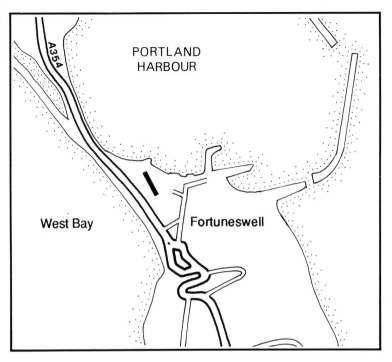

To the right in this picture can be seen RNAS Portland which covers a small area on the southern shore of Portland Harbour. *PRM*

Swordfish. The following year the squadron moved out and for the duration of the war Portland remained on C&M until, in 1946, the Anti-Submarine School returned with the Sikorsky R-4B helicopter, opening a new and still continuing chapter in the base's life story. Portland was commissioned as HMS *Osprey* in 1959 and fulfilled a training and trials role for the Royal Navy's helicopters and aircrews, together with an SAR commitment.

Today, the base undertakes helicopter maintenance for the FAA squadrons nominally based here, but whose helicopters are actually allocated to ships' Flights — namely Nos 702, 815 and 829 Squadrons — all of which operate the Lynx HAS3/3S in the anti-submarine warfare role; and No 772 Squadron operating the Sea King HC4 in the SAR role.

HMS *Osprey* usually has an annual open day/air show which affords the best opportunity to view the facilities.

ST MAWGAN

Cornwall (RAF) EGDG Tel: 0637 872201
OS Map Ref: SW86/63

High on the cliffs above Watergate Bay, RAF St Mawgan is also referred to as Newquay Airport for scheduled civil airline services by Brymon Airways. The airfield itself, and access to the military section, is north of the A3059 road and five miles east-northeast of Newquay. The civil aviation terminal is signposted on the minor road on the north side of the airfield, to the north of the single runway, 13/31, which is 9,006ft in length with a slight incline towards the middle.

Opened in 1943, St Mawgan's wartime life revolved around USAAF overseas transport flights with the B-24 and PB4Y-1 Liber-ator. BOAC and KLM aircraft also staged through here on some of their schedules. At the end of the war, St Mawgan was used as a staging point for USAAF and RCAF aircraft returning home across the Atlantic. The future of the station then became uncertain for several years until, in 1951, RAF Coastal Command's School of Maritime Reconnaissance became the first of several new arrivals, equipped with the Lancaster GR3. There followed a growing involvement for the station in Maritime Reconnaissance and Patrol work over the South Western Approaches and the Atlantic Ocean, witnessing a number of squadrons passing through which operated the Shackleton, and a Whirlwind-equipped SAR Flight. Changing

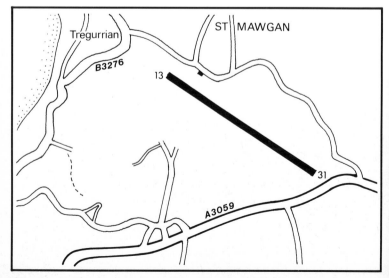

strategic priorities have resulted in Kinloss (qv) becoming the UK's premier maritime patrol base today, leaving St Mawgan with just two resident units.

These are No 42 Squadron and No 236 OCU, both of which operate in the maritime reconnaissance role with the long-range BAe Nimrod MR2/2P aircraft which patrol far out over the Atlantic Ocean. No 42 Squadron will disband from August 1992 and No 236 OCU will redeploy to Kinloss later in that year.

The School of Combat Survival and Rescue and No 3 Maritime Headquarters Unit will move here from Mountbatten by September 1992. Further roles are also being considered for St Mawgan.

Because of the incline towards the centre of the runway, the military aprons on the south side cannot be seen by the public from the airport terminal, although the Bulldog aircraft of various UAS which visit on summer camp tend to park on the civil aprons adjacent to the terminal.

SCAMPTON

Lincolnshire (RAF) EGXP Tel: 0522 730421
OS Map Ref: SK96/79
Famous for the exploits of its wartime squadrons, Scampton is situated five miles north of Lincoln. It is readily apparent on any road map for when runway 05/23 was extended eastwards to its present length of 8,990ft, it gave the A15 Ermine Street a distinctly pregnant appearance.

Opened in 1936 as a permanent station in Bomber Command, Scampton was built on the site of a World War 1 fighter aerodrome. During World War 2 the station won lasting fame as the erstwhile home of the legendary Dambusters — No 617 Squadron — although they were based here for only five months in 1943. The rest of the war saw eight bomber squadrons stationed at Scampton at varying times, their Hampdens, Manchesters and Lancasters engaged in the strategic air offensive against Germany. Postwar, the station's operational life was somewhat fragmented until, in 1953, a Canberra Bomber Wing was formed, staying at

Scampton is home to the RAF's premier aerobatic team the Red Arrows and its Hawk T1As. PRM

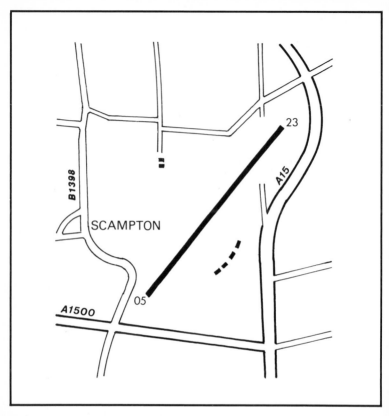

Scampton until 1955 when the station was closed for redevelopment as a V-Bomber base. Reopening in 1958, Scampton became home to a V-Bomber Wing equipped with the Avro Vulcan. However, Scampton's Vulcan days came to an end in 1982 and with it some 46 years of association with Bomber and Strike Commands. The station was then transferred to RAF Support Command and has since fulfilled a training function.

Today, the station is home to the RAF Central Flying School tasked with the training of instructors for all three Services and for other nations, too, with the Bulldog T1 and Tucano T1. The best-known and most admired advertisement for the RAF, the Red Arrows display team with its Hawk T1A aircraft, has been based here since 1984.

Also based here is the Trade Management Training School (TMTS) with a number of ground instructional airframes.

The Humber Gliding Club of the RAFGSA is also based here for recreational flying which takes place mostly at the weekend.

British Aerospace Plc has two small hangars of its own here, in the northwest corner of the site, with direct access from the minor road on the north side of the base. BAe undertakes work on Phantom aircraft in transit to or from its facility at Brough.

The eastward extension of the runway and the construction of an alternative A15 road had the advantage of leaving a dead-end stub on the south side of the runway, where it is safe to park. From here the aprons can be observed, but only with difficulty, and the movements recorded.

SHAWBURY

Shropshire (RAF) EGOS Tel: 0939 250351
OS Map Ref: SJ55/21

Shawbury is situated between the A49 to the west and the A53 to the east; to the west of the B5063, eight miles north-north-east of Shrewsbury. It has two runways: the main, 01/19, is 6,018 ft in length, and the subsidiary, 05/23, is 4,523ft in length.

Shawbury's origins can be traced back to 1917 when an RFC training airfield existed on the site, although it was not until 1938 that a redeveloped Shawbury reopened in its present form. During World War 2, basic flying training of RAF aircrews was undertaken here and the airfield also played host to a large maintenance unit, No 27. In 1944, the Central Navigation School arrived with a selection of different aircraft types, merging in 1950 with the School of Air Traffic Control to form the Central Navigation & Control School, retitled Central Air Traffic Control School in 1963. No 27 MU closed in 1972

and since then Shawbury has acted as the Central Flying School's rotary wing flying training base.

With the demise of the Central Air Traffic Control School in 1990, air activity at the base has been drastically reduced. Only the movements into and out of the storage site have increased, where a large number of RAF aircraft are mothballed.

No 2 FTS currently operates a fleet of Gazelle HT3 and Wessex HC2 helicopters during the daytime on weekdays. Nearby, Ternhill with its two runways is used as an RLG for helicopters only. No 8 AEF also operates the Chipmunk T10 from here.

Marshall of Cambridge (Engineering) Ltd has a maintenance base on site, which also services the RAF's Bulldog aircraft.

Views of the aprons east of the runways may be had from the B5063, north of the main gate, but these are poor.

Two blister-type hangars pictured at Shawbury, a typical maintenance unit airfield, with a Wessex in the foreground. *Paul Jackson*

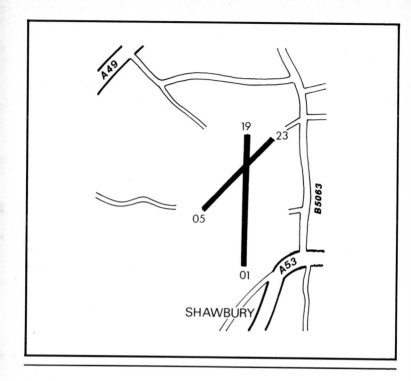

SYERSTON

Nottinghamshire (RAF) Tel: 0636 85467 OS
Map Ref: SK73/47

This airfield is trapped between the east
bank of the River Trent and the A46 road,
six miles southwest of Newark-on-Trent.
There are three concrete runways, but they
are not in general use.

Syerston opened in 1940 as a bomber
station in No 1 Group, one of the last prewar
Expansion Scheme permanent stations to
be completed. During the war years it saw
extensive use by a succession of six
squadrons flying the Wellington, Manchester
and Lancaster on bombing operations
against Germany. Postwar, the station
passed to Transport Command and then to
Flying Training Command in 1947, with
No 22 FTS tasked initially with the training
of FAA pilots on DH Tiger Moth and Percival
Prentice aircraft. From 1957, No 2 FTS
trained RAF pilots to fly with Piston and Jet
Provost aircraft. In 1971, No 2 FTS left
Syerston and the station was closed until in
1976 the RAF Central Gliding School
arrived.

Today, the RAF Air Cadets' Central Gliding School (ACCGS) (HQ at Newton, Notts)
is based here, from where it allocates and
maintains the gliders deployed to its Volunteer Gliding Schools nationwide. The
ACCGS has examples of all current powered and unpowered military glider types,
which include the Vigilant T1, Viking T1,
Janus C, Valiant TX1, Vanguard TX1 and
Venture T2. No 644 VGS is based here and
also operates these glider types.

The Four Counties Gliding Club of the
RAFGSA flies from here at weekends with
civil-registered gliders. Air Soaring (Oxford)
Ltd has facilities here which are connected
with the RAF's acquisition of the Vigilant T1
glider, assembled and test-flown from here
before acceptance.

There is also an RAF Police Dog School
active on this base — trespassers beware!

There is a short, rough track, on the out-

The Royal Air Force's first Vigilant is pictured in front of a Type J hangar at Syerston.
Paul Jackson

side of the northern boundary fence, west from the A46. Good views across the aprons can be gained from this track, and into-sun photographs attempted of taxying aircraft, and the landing movements.

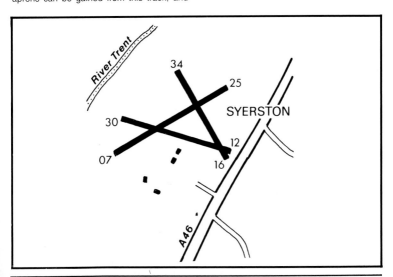

TEVERSHAM

Cambridgeshire (CIVIL) EGSC Tel: 0223 61133 OS Map Ref: TL49/59

This airfield is owned and operated by Marshall of Cambridge (Engineering) Ltd and also serves as Cambridge Airport for scheduled civil airline services. Some private general aviation aircraft are also based here. The airfield lies to the east of the A1134 road, south of the A1303, and some two miles east of Cambridge city centre. The airfield has two grass runways: 05/23, 2,936ft in length, and 10/28, 2,280ft in length; an asphalt runway runs parallel to grass runway 05/23, and is 6,447ft long. Parallel operations can take place from both runways.

Opened in 1929, Teversham's first residents were the Hawker Harts and Fairey Battles of No 22 ERFTS, and Marshall of Cambridge (Engineering) Ltd. In 1938 Cambridge Airport was opened on the site. Throughout World War 2, Marshall undertook a huge repair and overhaul function for the RAF: Whitleys, Oxfords, Stirlings, Mosquitoes, Spitfires and Typhoons, to name but a few, enjoyed its attention. Flying training also continued unabated with No 4 Flying Instructor's School and No 22 EFTS using a combination of Masters, Magisters, Tiger Moths and Austers. Renamed No 22 RFS, the latter unit remained at Teversham until disbandment in 1954.

The name of Marshall of Cambridge Ltd has been synonymous with the airfield since 1929, and remains so to this day. Postwar, it has been involved in contract maintenance and conversion work for the RAF, notably with the Venom, Brigand, Canberra, Valiant, Britannia and Hercules. A certain amount of development and fabrication work has also been undertaken over the years for BAC and its successor BAe. Today, Marshall undertakes MOD contract work on modifications to ex-airline TriStars, converting them to military K2 standard for the RAF. The company also works on the BAe 146 and MD-11 civil airliners, so the variety and size of aircraft to be seen here is varied and interesting. Maintenance work is carried out on C-130 Hercules aircraft, not only for the RAF but also for the overseas air forces of Sweden and Algeria.

Cambridge University Air Squadron operates its Bulldog T1 aircraft from Teversham (Cambridge Airport). *PRM*

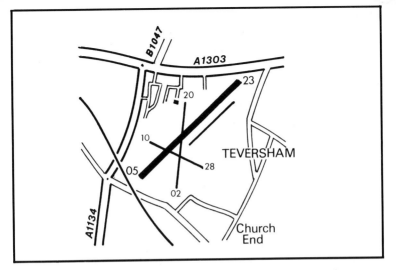

The based RAF presence at Teversham is limited to the Bulldog T1s of Cambridge UAS, and to the Chipmunk T10s of No 5 AEF. Government, military and corporate jet aircraft also visit the airport on business.

There is no general public access to the airport terminal, but the airfield can be viewed from the minor road to Cherry Hinton on the east side. The minor road to the south of the airfield affords photographic opportunities for runway 23 departures.

UPPER HEYFORD

Oxfordshire (USAFE) EGUA Tel: 0869 234808/234678 OS Map Ref: SP51/25
This busy base holds the high ground to the west of Junction 10 on the M40 motorway, 12 miles north of Oxford. Its single runway, 09/27, is 9,592ft long.

Upper Heyford's origins as an airfield go back as far as 1916, and in the closing months of World War 1 it was used by elements of the Canadian Air Force. The airfield was closed in 1920 and underwent major development, reopening as a bomber station in 1927. At the outbreak of war in 1939, Upper Heyford fulfilled a training function with No 6 Group Bomber Command and by April 1940 No 16 OTU was officially formed here to train bomber crews for the RAF. The unit remained here until March 1946, operating the Hampden, Hereford, Wellington and Mosquito. Postwar, the station hosted the Parachute Training School from 1946-50, and in 1951 the USAF assumed control. A major runway extension and the construction of new and specialised

buildings took place before the first residents, the 93rd Air Refueling Squadron and its Boeing KB-29Ps arrived. Thereafter, Upper Heyford acted as a home to the B-47 Stratojets of SAC until control of the base was transferred to USAFE in 1965. The following year saw the arrival of the 66th TRW with the RF-100C Voodoo, operating from the base until its replacement in 1970 by the 20th TFW and the F-111.

The 20th FW and the 66th Electronic Countermeasures Wing (ECW) are currently based here. The former has some 75 F-111E fighter-bomber aircraft divided between its three component squadrons: the 55th FS with blue fin markings, the 77th FS (red), and the 79th FS (yellow). The 42nd Electronic Countermeasures Squadron (ECS) of the 66th ECW has some 15 EF-111A Raven aircraft.

The EF-111A aircraft occupy the HAS complex at the west end of the base, north of the runway. The F-111E aircraft occupy the hangars and HAS south of the runway.

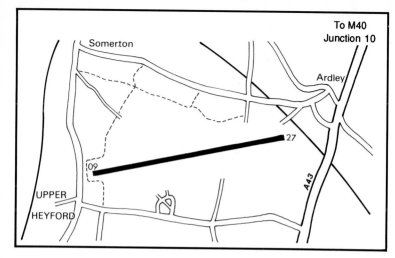

These aircraft all wear the base code letters UH on their tailplanes.

The Upper Heyford Flying Club has several civil-registered private aircraft for club members' use.

The height of the runway makes viewing difficult. Some aprons can be observed from the minor road between Upper Heyford village and the main gate, and from the no through-road remnant stub south of the runway. Viewing and photography of aircraft on approach to runway 27 is good from the dead-end road from Ardley village, north of the runway. There is a bridleway to Somerton along the west side of the base, and a public footpath along the northern boundary.

At almost 9,600ft in length, Upper Heyford's runway can — and does — cater for the largest aircraft. Visiting aircraft from other USAF and NATO units tend to park on a ramp among the hangars behind the main gate, and the lie of the land precludes these from being easily seen or photographed *in situ*.

VALLEY

Gwynedd (RAF) EGOV Tel: 0407 762241
OS Map Ref: SH30/76

RAF Valley is located in an isolated position on the southern shore of the Isle of Anglesey, between the Holyhead-Bangor railway line and Cymyran Bay, north of Rhosneigr. It has three runways: the main is 14/32, 7,513ft long; the two subsidiaries are 01/19, 5,381ft long, and 08/26, 4,200ft long.

Opened in 1941 as a Fighter Command sector station, Valley's various day and nightfighter squadrons were tasked with providing cover for Liverpool and the northwest of England during World War 2. Both the USAAF and the RAF used Valley from 1943 onwards as a ferry terminal for aircraft flying to the UK from the USA. With the end of the war, Valley acted as a ferry terminal in reverse and by 1947 it was put on C&M until 1951 when it came into its own as one of Flying Training Command's most important bases, which it remains to this day.

Valley's units currently perform two important tasks: No 4 FTS with a complement of some 50 Hawk T1/T1A jet trainers, trains Service pilots to fly during the weekday daylight hours; C Flight of No 22 Squadron, equipped with the Wessex HC2 helicopter, operates an all-weather SAR and Mountain Rescue facility. The SAR helicopters and more Hawks are based in the triangle north of runway 08 threshold and west of runway 14 threshold. These can be observed from the path that leads to the beach on the west side of the base, south from the village of Llanfair-yn-Neubwll.

There is an area for public parking and viewing on the west side of the railway,

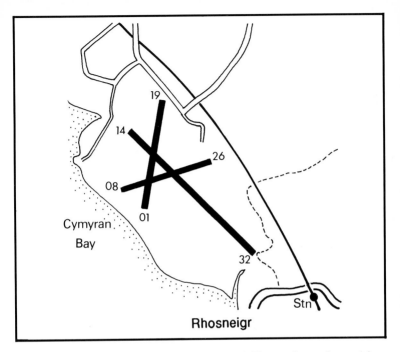

Cymyran
Bay

Rhosneigr

close to the overbridge on the minor road from the A5 through Llanfihangel-yn-Nhowyn village. From here the Hawks on the aprons east of runway 01/19 can be observed. Photography can be good from the footpath at the southern end of the base, east of and near to the threshold of runway 32, towards Rhosneigr.

WADDINGTON

Lincolnshire (RAF) EGXW Tel: 0522 720271
OS Map Ref: SK97/64

Another Lincolnshire airfield with an illustrious war record, Waddington lies between the A607 road in the west and the A15 to the east, about four miles south of the city of Lincoln. It has a single 9,000ft runway, 03/21.

Opened in 1916 as a flying training station for the RFC, Waddington closed in 1919 only to reopen in 1926 as a bomber station. During the 1930s it was extensively rebuilt as part of the RAF's prewar Expansion Scheme and at the outbreak of war came under the operational control of Bomber Command in No 5 Group. World War 2 saw Waddington play an active part in the strategic bomber offensive against Germany. Nine frontline bomber squadrons were stationed here at various times during the war, operating the Hampden, Manchester and Lancaster. Postwar, Waddington remained with Bomber Command, its squadrons operating the Lincoln, from 1957 V-Force Vulcans, and ultimately Vulcan K2 tankers until the type was finally withdrawn from RAF service in 1984. Waddington was temporary host to the short-lived Nimrod AEW3 Joint Training Unit in 1985 and also operated a Shackleton major servicing facility. NATO E-3A AWACS aircraft were regular visitors here up until 1991 when No 8 Squadron moved in from Lossiemouth (qv) with its new E-3D Sentry AEW1 aircraft.

There are two resident units at Waddington today. No 8 Squadron and its E-3D Sentry aircraft is the sole operational unit, fulfilling an airborne early warning role which,

Britain's AEW requirement is now covered by No 8 Squadron and its Boeing E-3D AEW1 aircraft based at Waddington. *Brian Strickland*

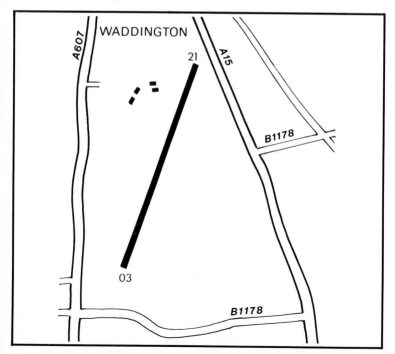

until recently, was operated by the squadron's venerable Shackleton AEW2s from Lossiemouth. The newly acquired E-3Ds occupy a recently prepared facility on the west side of the runway at the north end. The Vulcan Display Flight is the other resident unit, operating the sole flying Vulcan B2, XH558.

The main gate, with a Vulcan acting as a gate guardian, is on the A607 road, near to the hangar complex. General viewing and photography are better from the A15 on the base's east side.

The BAe North Sea Range, opened in 1991, has attracted many British units and overseas' air forces as customers. These aircraft frequently recover to Waddington and night-/weekend-stop, in the open, east of the runway.

WARTON

Lancashire (CIVIL) EGNO Tel: 0772 852374
OS Map Ref: SD40/27

Warton lies on the north bank of the Ribble Estuary, eight miles west of Preston and south of the A584 road. It has two runways: the main, 08/26, is 7,946ft long, and the subsidiary, 14/32, is 4,209ft long. It is on this that visiting night-stopping large aircraft frequently park.

Opened in 1943 under the control of the USAAF, Warton became home to No 2 Base Air Depot specialising in the overhaul and modification of almost 10,000 US aircraft in its two years of operation. Postwar, it was returned to the RAF and became home to No 90 MU until the early 1950s when the aircraft manufacturer English Electric acquired the airfield for test-flying the Canberra and P1A (Lightning). Latterly, BAC and its successor BAe have test-flown and built the Jaguar and Tornado here.

Today, Warton is owned and operated by British Aerospace Plc Military Aircraft Division, and is used for the production and

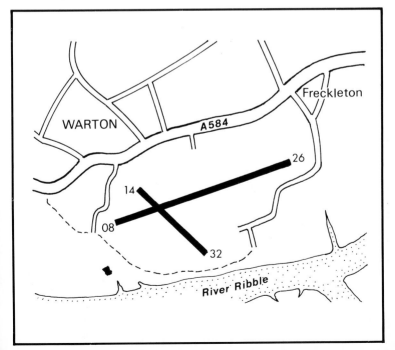

flight-testing of all Tornado variants for the RAF and export customers, including Saudi Arabia. The manufacturing shops are to the north of the runway and the flight testing facility is on the south side of the runway, at the western end. Also based here is the BAe Experimental Aircraft Programme (EAP) technology demonstrator, several company Lightning F6 aircraft with overwing tanks and a handful of company civil-registered business aircraft.

The best views of the aprons are obtained from the minor road, signposted to a caravan site, to Warton Bank at the west end of the site. To observe or photograph operations on runway 26, it is best to get to the south of the runway on the minor road to Naze Mount, by leaving Freckleton village, on the A584, on Naze Lane East. There is a public footpath between Warton Bank and Naze Lane East through the marshes, round the south side of the airfield.

Because of the sensitive nature of BAe's business activities and the involvement of other nations, the company's security staff are quite reasonably vigilant and highly reactive to the presence of, or any interest shown by, unauthorised persons. Members of the public are not given access to the site on Family Days, either.

WATTISHAM

Suffolk (RAF) EGUW Tel: 0449 720631 OS Map Ref: TM03/51
This airfield is camouflaged into the East Anglian landscape 10 miles northwest of Ipswich, to the north of the B1078 road. It has one runway, 05/23, which is 7,490ft long.

Wattisham opened in 1939 as one of the last prewar Expansion Scheme airfields to be completed. It hosted five Blenheim light

The control tower at Wattisham keeps a close eye on a visiting Czechoslovak Air Force MiG-29. *Paul Jackson*

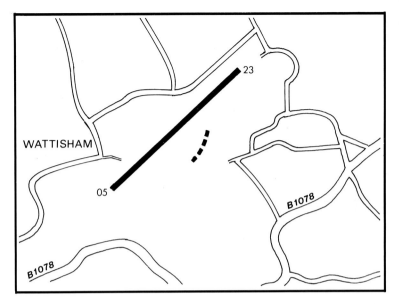

WATTISHAM

23

05

B1078

B1078

bomber squadrons under No 2 Group control until, in September 1942, the USAAF assumed control of the station. Used initially as an aircraft depot, Wattisham saw action towards the war's end as a US fighter base operating the P-38 Lightning and P-51 Mustang. The station returned to RAF control postwar. Considerably updated, since then it has hosted a number of air defence fighter squadrons using the Meteor, Hunter, Lightning and latterly the F-4J Phantom.

Today, No 56 Squadron operates from the HAS complex on the south side of the runway, flying about 20 Phantom FGR2s in the air defence role. Fourteen of the latest version — the F-4J(UK) which were ex-US Navy aircraft, modified to RAF standards —

equipped No 74 Squadron which was housed in HAS on the north side of the runway, opposite the aprons of the original hangars. All of this version have now been withdrawn from active service.

Both Phantom squadrons are due to be disbanded: No 56 by October 1992 and No 74 by April 1993. Wattisham will then close as a station but may be retained as an Air Defence Forward Operating Base.

The Anglia Gliding Club of the RAFGSA flies from here at weekends and from 1800hrs until dusk on Fridays.

Minor roads surround most of the base and from these various views of the aprons can be obtained.

WITTERING

Cambridgeshire (RAF) EGXT Tel: 0780 64501 OS Map Ref: TF04/02
Wittering lies to the west of the A1(T) dual carriageway, within the A1/A43/A47 triangle, about three miles south of Stamford. The present day-base is, in fact, a merger of the original 1916 Wittering airfield with the 1940 Collyweston airfield at the west end. The single runway, 08/26, is 9,050ft long and links the two. The Collyweston end is now

used mainly as the dump and for fire practice.

Wittering can trace its origins back to World War 1 when it was known as Stamford and was used as a training airfield by the RFC. With its name changed to Wittering in 1924, the Central Flying School (CFS) moved in and remained here until 1935 when Wittering became a fighter base. Throughout World War 2 the station's suc-

A Gaydon hangar at Wittering with Harrier GR5s in the foreground. *Paul Jackson*

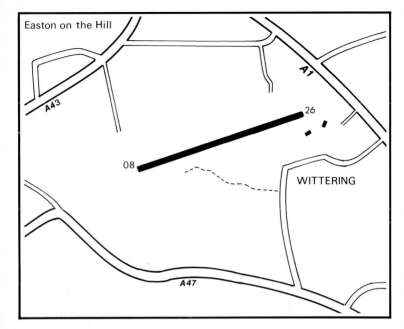

cession of squadrons flew day and night-fighter sorties using a variety of aircraft ranging from the Spitfire, Hurricane, Defiant and Beaufighter to the Turbinlite Havoc and Mosquito. Postwar, control passed to Flying Training Command in 1948 and then to Bomber Command in 1953 when Wittering became a V-Force base flying Valiants. In 1969, the station reverted to the fighter role with the arrival of No 1 Squadron, the first RAF squadron to operate the STOVL Harrier.

Today, Wittering is the sole UK home to the RAF's Harrier force. No 233 OCU is based here with a mixture of Harrier T4 two-seaters and GR3/5A aircraft, with a single-letter tail code, prefixed with the digit 3 in the case of the GR3 aircraft. From Septem-ber 1992, the unit will bear the shadow designation of No 20 Squadron, following the disbandment of No 20 Squadron at Laar-bruch, Germany.

No 1 Squadron occupies the large hangar and apron nearest to the A1 road from where it operates the Harrier GR5A/GR7.

The aprons outside the hangars can be partially observed from the minor road through Wittering village on the south side of the airfield, and from the private road to Easton Lodge Farm which leads off it.

The A1(T) dual carriageway is not recom-mended for parking or stopping, but never-theless is a good site for photography of air-craft on finals to runway 26, if you can find somewhere safe to park and walk.

WOODBRIDGE

Suffolk (USAFE) EGVG Tel: 0394 433737
OS Map Ref: TM32/47
Woodbridge airfield is inconspicuously hid-den in Rendlesham Forest, 10 miles east-northeast of Ipswich, in the arc between the B1084 and the B1083 roads. It has a single runway, 09/27, which is 9,000ft long.

Woodbridge opened on 15 November 1943 as one of three emergency diversion airfields down the east coast of England (the other two were Carnaby, Yorkshire, and Manston, Kent). Each had a 3,000yd-long runway, 250yd-wide with under and over-shoots of 500yd at each end. For aircraft

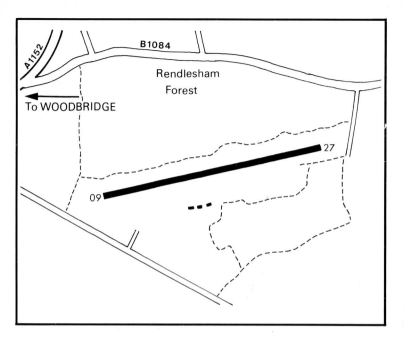

that were badly damaged, lost or short of fuel, these airfields provided a huge emergency runway equipped with FIDO and full approach and airfield lighting, giving it an all-weather capability. By the war's end, over 4,000 emergency landings had been made at Woodbridge. Postwar, the station was used for experimental work and the RAF relinquished its control in March 1948. In June 1952, the USAF assumed control of Woodbridge, its first residents being the F-84G Thunderstreaks and F-100 Super Sabres of the 20th Fighter Bomber Wing's (FBW) 79th Fighter Bomber Squadron (FBS) which remained here until 1969. The 81st TFW took over control of Woodbridge in July 1958 and the 78th TFS moved in at the end of the year with its F-84s and F-100s, converting to the F-4 Phantom in 1966. In December 1969, the 67th Aerospace Rescue & Recovery Squadron (ARRS) arrived with the HC-130 Hercules and the HH-3E Jolly Green Giant helicopter. The year 1988 saw the 67th ARRS reorganised to form the 21st and 67th Special Operations Squadrons (SOS) under the control of the 39th Special Operations Wing (SOW), tasked with long-range rescue duties.

Today, Woodbridge is operated by USAFE and is the 'twin' base with nearby Bentwaters (qv). Two of the four squadrons which comprise the 81st FW based at Bentwaters operate the A-10A Thunderbolt from the HAS complex on the southside of Woodbridge's runway. The 78th FS, with red tailfin-tip markings, and the 91st FS with blue markings, all wear the base code-letters WR on their tails. The 81st FW started to send its A-10s elsewhere in the spring of 1992 and by 1993 will have lost its entire complement of 80 aircraft. Once the USAF has moved out, Woodbridge will then be closed to flying from the autumn of 1992, its future uncertain.

The 39th SOW currently controls two squadrons with aircraft based here. The 67th SOS operates the HC-130N Hercules and two HC-130P Hercules as rescue command posts in conjunction with other AWACS aircraft. The 21st SOS operates four MH-53J 'Pave Low III' helicopters. (The 27th and 67th SOS relocated their operations to Alconbury in the summer of 1992.) These and the Hercules are usually to be found on the aprons west of the main gate, which is on the north side of the minor road from the B1083 to Hollesley village.

There is a track into the forest at the west

end from which these aprons may be observed. Gale damage and tree felling have considerably thinned the forest on the north side of the runway, and it is possible to see across most of the airfield from tracks close to the boundary fence on the north side.

The best places for parking, observing and photographing aircraft on approach to runway 27 is on the south side of the run-way, at the east end, near an access gate by which pilots perform final checks prior to departing. This spot is reached southwards along a track from the B1084 road.

From this spot it is possible to stumble westwards through the gorse, heather and bracken, along the perimeter fence, and observe the aprons and HAS used by the resident A-10As, towards the main gate.

WYTON

Cambridgeshire (RAF) EGUY Tel: 0480 52451 OS Map Ref: TL28/73
This airfield lies to the east of the intersection of the B1090 road with the A141, four miles northeast of Huntingdon. It has a single runway, 09/27, which is 8,255ft long.

Although Wyton's history as an airfield stretches back to 1916, the present day station owes much to the rebuilding of the pre-war Expansion Scheme. Opening in 1936, Wyton served as a bomber station with a Blenheim of resident No 139 Squadron flying the first sortie of the war, on 3 September 1939. Between 1939-45, Wyton saw 10 separate squadron movements and witnessed a variety of its resident bomber aircraft types in action against the enemy, such as the Battle, Blenheim, Wellington, Stirling, Lancaster and Mosquito. The Pathfinder Force, redesignated No 8 (PFF) Group, was formed at Wyton in August 1942 and its HQ remained here until June 1943.

Postwar, Wyton remained as a bomber station until, in 1952, it became home for the RAF's strategic reconnaissance squadrons flying a mixture of Spitfires, Mosquitoes and Lancasters, later to be replaced by the Canberra, Valiant and Victor. Today, the station

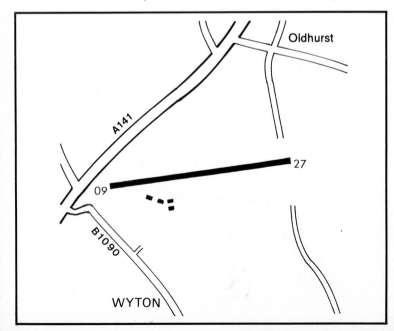

is the main home to the RAF's veteran Canberra fleet, many of which are currently being withdrawn and replaced by Hawk T1s.

Various versions of the Canberra serve with four RAF squadrons in different roles: No 231 OCU (B2, B2T, T4); No 1 PRU (PR9); No 100 Squadron (B2, E15, PR7, and TT18 for target-towing facilities); and No 360 Squadron (T17, T17A, for electronic countermeasures).

Three Nimrod R1P aircraft are based here with No 51 Squadron for electronic surveillance 'lead and mislead' duties, although these aircraft are sometimes deployed elsewhere, for example Akrotiri (Cyprus).

The four C-Type hangars and aprons are on the south side of the runway, with the main gate on the B1090 road. Many based aircraft park on the field and can be observed from the perimeter roads (A141 and B1090). The original road between St Ives and Oldhurst was severed when the runway was extended eastwards, the remaining dead-ends on each side affording views across the field and offering good photographic opportunities for aircraft on approach to runway 27.

YEOVILTON

Somerset HMS *Heron* (RN) EGDY Tel: 0935 840551; 0935 840565 (Museum) OS Map Ref: ST55/24
RNAS Yeovilton is south from the A303 Ilchester bypass, to the south of the B3151, five miles north of Yeovil. It has two runways: 09/27 is the main, and 7,521ft long; the subsidiary, 04/22, is 4,797ft long. There is also a 'Dummy Deck' with an inclined launching ramp left of runway 27 threshold.

Commissioned in 1939 as HMS *Heron*, Yeovilton's role during World War 2 was as a fighter training school for the FAA and as an occasional shore base for disembarked frontline squadrons, or those working up before embarking on carriers. Aircraft types to be seen here during World War 2 included the Master, Roc, Sea Gladiator, Sea Hurricane, Spitfire, Fulmar, Martlet and Firefly. Postwar, the station's role in naval

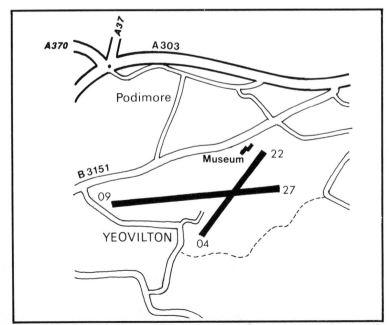

aviation expanded considerably when it became shore base for the fleet's all-weather fighters, with the Sea Vixen and latterly the F-4 Phantom. However, by 1972 Yeovilton's involvement with fixed-wing aviation came to a temporary close and a number of Commando helicopter squadrons were the only resident flying units. Things looked up in 1979 when the first STOVL Sea Harrier FRS1 aircraft arrived at Yeovilton, together with Sea King commando helicopters.

Today, Yeovilton is the shore base of the FAA's Sea Harrier aircraft and helicopters which deploy aboard the Royal Navy's three aircraft carriers. This is a vibrant base with many different aircraft types allocated to a number of units. The Fleet Requirements & Air Direction Unit (FRADU) operates a mixture of Canberra TT18 and Hunter T7, T8C and GA11 jet aircraft.

No 707 Squadron operates the Sea King HC4 commando helicopter in the Aircrewman & Officer Flying Training role. Nos 845 and 846 Squadrons also operate the Sea King HC4, but in the Commando & Amphibious Forces Support role.

No 899 Squadron's role is Fighter Reconnaissance & Strike, and operates the STOVL Sea Harrier FRS1, the Harrier T4N trainer and the Hunter T8M. The Sea Harrier FRS1 aircraft are allocated to No 800 Squadron of HMS *Invincible*, and to No 801

Squadron of HMS *Invincible*, which are shore-based here when not embarked.

No 3 Commando Brigade Air Squadron of the Royal Marines is also based here, operating some six Gazelle AH1 helicopters, and six TOW-Lynx AH1 helicopters in B Flight, which deploy aboard assault ships.

There are a couple of Chipmunk T10s with the Station Flight for communications duties and the remnants of the RN Historic Aircraft Flight are also based here although, sadly, the Flight is now disbanded.

The Heron Gliding Club of the RNGSA operates a variety of civil glider types from here at the weekends.

The other big attraction at Yeovilton is the Fleet Air Arm Museum and its newer limb the Concorde Hall, with a collection of about 60 different historic aircraft. The museum is open during the day, everyday, from where there are good views of the operational aprons of the Sea Harriers and Hunters.

The plethora of aprons around the small hangars can be observed through the jet efflux from the B3151 road on the north side. The minor roads at east and west ends permit views across the airfield and give photographic opportunities for aircraft on approach to the two runways. East from Yeovilton village, there is a bridleway close to the boundary fence which allows further viewing.

Yeovilton is the shore base of the FAA's Sea Harrier aircraft. Sea Harrier FRS1s of 800 Squadron (illustrated) are allocated to HMS *Invincible*. PRM

AIRFIELDS GUIDE

In this section, brief notes of the locations and users of active bases not fully covered earlier are given. Excluded are MOD sites with only static airframes, museums and civil airfields which may have based at them privately-owned aircraft still wearing military markings.

ABERPORTH, Dyfed
North of A487, east of B4333, six miles ENE of Cardigan. MOD PE (RAE).
Tel: 0239 810205.

ANDOVER, Hants
South of A303, two miles west of town. AAC. RLG for Middle Wallop (qv).

ARBROATH, Tayside
East of A933, two miles northwest of town. RAF. No 663 VGS with Viking gliders.

BARKSTON HEATH, Lincs
West by B6404, south of A153, six miles northeast of Grantham. RAF. RLG for Cranwell (qv). Tel: 0400 30621.

BEDFORD, Beds
On A6(T) and A428, 20 miles northeast of Milton Keynes. MOD PE (RAE). Large variety of aircraft on test and evaluation. Tel: 0234 270077.

BICESTER, Oxon
East by A421, one mile northeast of town, 14 miles northeast of Oxford. RAFGSA Centre, gliders and powered aerotows.

BINBROOK, Lincs
North of B1203, 10 miles SSW of Grimsby. RAF. No 643 VGHS with Viking T1 gliders. LG for Scampton (qv).
Tel: 0522 730421.

BISHOPS COURT, Co Down, NI
North of A2, six miles east of Downpatrick. RAF. No 664 VGS with Viking gliders.

BOULMER, Northumberland
East of B1339, four miles east of Alnwick. RAF. A Flight No 202 Sqn, Sea King SAR helicopters. Tel: 0665 604760.

BROUGH, Humberside
South of A63, on north bank of Humber estuary, six miles west of Hull. BAe. Construction of Pilatus PC-9 trainer. Tel: 0482 666900.

CATTERICK, N Yorks
East by A1, five miles southeast of Richmond. RAF. No 645 VGS with Viking gliders.

COSFORD, Salop
South of A41, north of A464, eight miles northwest of Wolverhampton. RAF. Birmingham UAS Bulldog T1 aircraft; No 633 VGS with Vigilant powered gliders; RAFGSA Wrekin Gliding Club; No 2 SoTT; Aerospace Museum.
SoTT tel: 0902 372393;
Museum tel: 0902 374872.

DISHFORTH, N Yorks
East by A1, south of A168, eight miles southwest of Thirsk. RAF. RAFGSA Cleveland Gliding Club. Tel: 0347 4261.

DUNSFOLD, Surrey
South of B2130, west of A281, eight miles south of Guildford. BAe. Construction of Harrier and Hawk aircraft.
Tel: 0483 272121.

EXETER, Devon
South by A30, east from M5 Jct 29, four miles east of Exeter. Civil airport. RAF. No 4 AEF based with Chipmunk T10 aircraft. Tel: 0392 68368 (RAF).

FAIRFORD, Glos
On A417, eight miles east of Cirencester. USAFE. Reserve base. Used by infrequent deployments. Tel: 0638 512942.

FLEETLANDS, Hants
East by A32, one mile south of Fareham. RN. Helicopter maintenance base.

GLASGOW, Strathclyde
North from M8 Jct 28, six miles west of Glasgow. Civil international airport. RAF. Glasgow & Strathclyde UAS based with Bulldog T1 aircraft. Tel: 041 887 1111/8918.

GREENHAM COMMON, Berks
North of A339, two miles southeast of Newbury. USAFE. Missile base and occasional fixed-wing visitors.
Tel: 0635 512043.

HALTON, Bucks
Between A4011 and B489, four miles southeast of Aylesbury. RAF. No 613 VGS with Vigilant T1 powered-gliders; RAFGSA Chilterns GC; No 1 SoTT. Tel: 0296 623535.

HENLOW, Beds
Between A600 and A6001, four miles north of Hitchin. RAF. No 616 VGS with Vigilant T1-powered gliders.

HULLAVINGTON, Wilts
West of A429, north from M4 Jct 17, east of village. RAFGSA Bannerdown GC. Due to close late 1992.

A number of airframe hulks are kept at Manston for use in fire control training. *Paul Jackson.*

KEMBLE, Wilts
North by A429, south of A433, five miles southwest of Cirencester. RAF. Storage and USAFE Logistics Command maintenance facility (due to leave by mid-1992).
Tel: 0285 770261.

KENLEY, Surrey
West of A22, east of B2030, two miles northwest of Caterham. RAF. No 615 VGS with Viking gliders.

KIRKNEWTON, Lothian
East by B7031, between A70 and A71, 10 miles southwest of Edinburgh. RAF. No 661 VGS with Viking gliders.

LECONFIELD, Humberside
East of A164, three miles north of Beverley. RAF. E Flight No 202 Sqn with Sea King SAR helicopters. Tel: 0964 550386.

LITTLE RISSINGTON, Gloucs
West of A424, five miles NNW of Burford. RAF. No 637 VGS with Viking gliders.

LLANBEDR, Gwynedd
By the shore of Cardigan Bay, west of town on A496, nine miles north of Barmouth. MOD PE (RAE). Test aircraft for Jindivik missile. Tel: 03412 3321.

MACHRIHANISH, Strathclyde
On west side of Kintyre peninsula, west of A83, three miles WNW of Campbeltown. RAF. Test aircraft. Some scheduled civil flights. Tel: 0586 53021.

MANSTON, Kent
Between A253 and B2050/2190, three miles west of Ramsgate. RAF. No 1 AEF with Chipmunk T10 aircraft; No 617 VGS with Viking gliders; C Flight No 202 Sqn with Sea King SAR helicopters; Memorial Pavilion. Tel: 0843 823351 (RAF).

MONA, Gwynedd
North by A5 on Anglesey, three miles west of Llangefni. RAF. RLG for Valley (qv); some private civil aircraft based.
Tel: 0407 720583.

NEWTON, Notts
North by A52, west by A46, seven miles east of Nottingham. RAF. East Midlands UAS with Bulldog T1 aircraft; No 7 AEF with Chipmunk T10 aircraft. Tel: 0949 20771.

OAKINGTON, Cambs
East of B1050, off A604, six miles northwest of Cambridge. AAC. No 657 Sqn with Lynx helicopters.

PLYMOUTH, Devon
East by A386, four miles north of city. Civil airport. RN Flying Grading Flight with Chipmunk aircraft. Tel: 0752 772752/3.

PREDANNACK, Cornwall
West by A3083, south of B3296, five miles south of Culdrose (qv), towards Lizard Point. RN. Fire School and satellite for Culdrose. RAF. No 626 VGS with Viking gliders. Tel: 0326 574121.

PRESTWICK (Navy), Strathclyde
HMS *Gannet*. South by B739, one mile east of Monkton village. RN. Nos 819 and 824 Sqns based on north side with Sea King helicopters; intermittent visiting military aircraft; international civil airport on south side; BAe construction of Jetstream aircraft; BAe Flying College Ltd. Tel: 0292 75000.

St ATHAN, South Glam
North of B4265, seven miles west of Barry, 12 miles WSW of Cardiff. RAF. Wales UAS Bulldog T1 and No 634 VGS with Viking gliders; Civilian Technical Training School; airframes and Museum store.
Tel: 0446 798798.

SAMLESBURY, Lancs
Between A677 and A59, two miles east of M6 Jct 31. BAe factory. RAF. No 635 VGS with Vigilant T1-powered gliders.

SCULTHORPE, Norfolk
North by A148, three miles west of Fakenham. USAFE. Reserve base; used by infrequent deployments. Tel: 03283 141419.

SEALAND, Clwyd
West by A550, five miles west of Chester. RAF. No 631 VGS with Viking gliders.

SOUTH CERNEY, Glos
South by A419, two miles southeast of Cirencester. RAF. No 625 VGS with Viking gliders.

SWANSEA, W Glam
West from A4118, six miles west of Swansea. Civil airport. RAF. No 636 VGS with Viking gliders. Tel: 0792 204063.

SWANTON MORLEY, Norfolk
Northwest of village on B1147, three miles northeast of East Dereham. RAF. No 611 VGS with Viking gliders. Central Servicing Development Establishment.

The distinctive blister hangar and factory at St Athan form a dramatic backdrop as a Jaguar taxies along the runway. *Paul Jackson*

SWINDERBY, Lincs
East by A46, eight miles southwest of
Lincoln. RAF. RAF EFTS With Chipmunk
T10. ELG. Tel: 0522 86421.

SYDENHAM, Co Down, NI
East side of Belfast Docks, two miles east of
city centre. Shorts Plc, Tucano factory.
Belfast City/Harbour Airport (Tel: 0232
458444). RAF. Queen's UAS with Bulldog
T1 aircraft, No 13 AEF with Chipmunk T10
aircraft.

TERNHILL, Salop
West by A41, east of A53, 15 miles
northeast of Shrewsbury. RAF. No 632 VGS
with Vigilant powered gliders. RLG for
Shawbury. Tel: 0939 250351.

THURLEIGH, Beds
Between A6 and B660, six miles north of
Bedford. MOD PE (RAE). Various aircraft
types for experimental work.

TOPCLIFFE, N Yorks
East of A167, five miles southwest of Thirsk.
AAC. No 3 Flt with Gazelle helicopters;
No 657 Sqn with the Lynx and Gazelle
helicopters. RN EFTS with the Bulldog T1.
RLG for Linton-on-Ouse (qv). Tel: 0748
832521.

TURNHOUSE, Lothian
North from A8, five miles west of Edinburgh.
north side of runway 13/31 Edinburgh
Airport. RAF. E Lowlands UAS with Bulldog
aircraft and No 12 AEF with Chipmunk T10
aircraft. Used by occasional USAF/USN
deployments. Tel: 031 339 5393.

UPAVON, Wilts
South by A342, 14 miles west of Andover.
RAF. HQ No 1 Grp Strike Command;
No 622 VGS with Viking gliders; AGA
Wyvern GC. Tel: 0980 630351.

WEST FREUGH, Dumfries & Galloway
Between A715 and A757, five miles
southeast of Stranraer. MOD PE (RAE).
Testing of aircraft. Tel: 0776 2501.

WEST MALLING, Kent
North of A26, east of A228, south of village,
five miles west of Maidstone. RAF. No 618
VGS with Viking gliders.

WESTON-ON-THE-GREEN, Oxon
Between A43 and A421, eight miles north of
Oxford. RAF Sport Parachute Association.

WETHERSFIELD, Essex
East of B1053, six miles northwest of
Braintree. RAF. No 614 VGS with Viking
gliders. USAFE reserve base.

WOODVALE, Merseyside
West of A565, six miles southwest of
Southport. RAF. Liverpool and Manchester
UASs with Bulldog T1 aircraft; No 10 AEF
with Chipmunk T10 aircraft; some civil
aircraft also based. Tel: 07048 72287.

WROUGHTON, Wilts
East of A361, three miles south of Swindon.
AAC/RN helicopter store; Science Museum
Air Transport Collection; periodic civil
aircraft fly-ins.

YEOVIL, Somerset
Between A30 and A3008, west of town.
Westlands Plc. Helicopter production. Tel:
0935 75222.

ADDENDA

As identified in the Introduction, the RAF is
undergoing a significant reorganisation, in
order to operate within the new strategic sit-
uation of the 1990s.

During the production of this book there
have been a number of changes to be
noted.

Aldergrove: Now home to 72/230
Squadrons (Wessex/Puma).
Benson: No 60 Squadron formed 1/6/92
with Wessex HC2s.
Brawdy: No 79 Squadron disbanded
31/8/92.
Chivenor: No 92 (Reserve) Squadron
reformed 1/9/92, replacing No 151
Squadron, disbanded 30/8/92.

Church Fenton: No 7FTS disbanded
1/4/92, reforming at Chivenor.
Coningsby: No 65 (Reserve) Squadron
disbanded 1/7/92.
Lossiemouth: No 208 Squadron to disband
1/4/92.
Marham: No 27 Squadron disbanded
1/10/92 to become 'shadow' of No 240
OCU at Odiham. No 55 Squadron to
become shadow of No 241 OCU on
1/1/93.
St Mawgan: No 42 Squadron disbanded
10/92, No 236 OCU will redeploy to
Kinloss late in 1992.
Wattisham: No 56 Squadron disbanded
6/92. No 74 Squadron replaced No 3
Training School at No 4 FTS, Valley, on
1/10/92.
Wyton: No 1 PRM reformed 1/7/92 with
No 39 (Reserve) Squadron.

BIBLIOGRAPHY

P. Calvocoressi, *World Politics Since 1945*, (3rd Ed), (Longman, 1977)

M. Dewar, *Defence of the Nation* (Arms & Armour Press, 1989)

Wg Cdr C.G. Jefford, *RAF Squadrons* (Airlife, 1988)

David J. Smith, *Britain's Military Airfields 1939-45*, (Patrick Stephens Ltd, 1989)

Steve Willis and Barry Holliss, *Military Airfields of the British Isles 1939-45*, (Enthusiasts Publications, 1989)

Action Stations, various volumes and authors (Patrick Stephens Ltd)

RAF Flight Information Publication: British Isles & North Atlantic En Route Supplement – September 1991 (RAF 1 AIDU)

Aviation News, various issues

British Aviation Review (British Aviation Research Group), various issues

The Times, various issues

Ulster Airmail (Ulster Aviation Society), various issues

Harrier GR5 ZD378 stands, appropriately, in front of the new Harrier engineering hangar at Wittering. The hangar has concertina doors specifically tailored to the Harrier. *Paul Jackson*

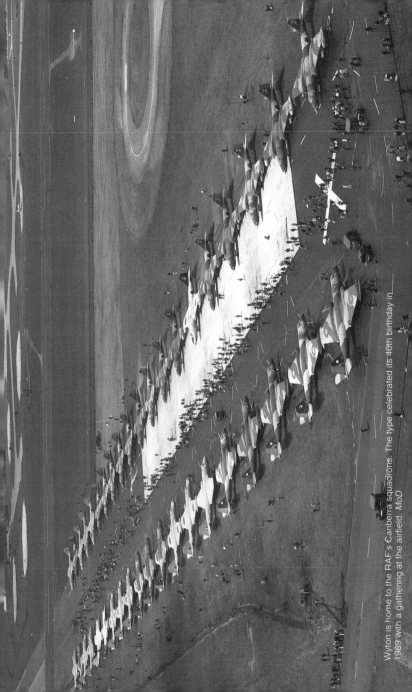

Wyton is home to the RAF's Canberra squadrons. The type celebrated its 40th birthday in 1989 with a gathering at the airfield. *MoD*